Free DVD   FREE   Free DVD

Essential Test Tips Video from Trivium Test Prep

Dear Customer,

Thank you for purchasing from Trivium Test Prep! Whether you're looking to join the military, get into college, or advance your career, we're honored to be a part of your journey.

To show our appreciation (and to help you relieve a little of that test-prep stress), we're offering a **FREE *NEX Essential Test Tips* Video** by Trivium Test Prep. Our video includes 35 test preparation strategies that will help keep you calm and collected before and during your big exam. All we ask is that you email us your feedback and describe your experience with our product. Amazing, awful, or just so-so: we want to hear what you have to say!

To receive your **FREE *NEX Essential Test Tips* Video**, please email us at 5star@triviumtestprep.com. Include "Free 5 Star" in the subject line and the following information in your email:

1. The title of the product you purchased.
2. Your rating from 1 – 5 (with 5 being the best).
3. Your feedback about the product, including how our materials helped you meet your goals and ways in which we can improve our products.
4. Your full name and shipping address so we can send your **FREE *NEX Essential Test Tips* Video**.

If you have any questions or concerns please feel free to contact us directly at 5star@triviumtestprep.com.

Thank you, and good luck with your studies!

NEX Study Guide

2 Practice Exams and NLN NEX Test Prep

Jeremy Downs

Copyright ©2024 Trivium Test Prep

ISBN-13: 9781637987186

ALL RIGHTS RESERVED. By purchase of this book, you have been licensed on copy for personal use only. No part of this work may be reproduced, redistributed, or used in any form or by any means without prior written permission of the publisher and copyright owner. Trivium Test Prep; Accepted, Inc.; Cirrus Test Prep; and Ascencia Test Prep are all imprints of Trivium Test Prep, LLC.

TABLE OF CONTENTS

Introduction i

Verbal Skills 1
    Reading Comprehension 1
    Vocabulary 9
    Answer Key 14

Mathematics 15
    Types of Numbers 15
    Decimals and Fractions 19
    Converting Between Fractions and Decimals 21
    Rounding and Estimation 22
    Ratios 22
    Proportions 23
    Percentages 23
    Percent Change 24
    Comparison of Rational Numbers 25
    Algebraic Expressions 25
    Operations with Expressions 26
    Distributing and Factoring 26
    Linear Equations 27
    Graphs of Linear Equations 27
    Building Equations 28
    Inequalities 29
    Units of Measurement 30
    Statistics 31
    Data Presentation 33
    Answer Key 37

Anatomy and Physiology 50
    Anatomical Terminology 50
    The Respiratory System 53

The Cardiovascular System	54
The Nervous System	57
The Gastrointestinal System	61
The Skeletal System	62
The Muscular System	65
Muscle Cell Structure	66
The Immune System	68
The Reproductive System	70
The Endocrine System	72
The Integumentary System	74
The Genitourinary System	76
Answer Key	77

Biology *79*

Biological Macromolecules	79
The Cell	82
Genetics	86
Answer Key	88

Chemistry *90*

Properties of Atoms	90
Intramolecular Bonds	98
Intermolecular Bonds	100
Properties of Substances	101
States of Matter	103
Chemical Reactions	105
Catalysts	108
Acids and Bases	110
Answer Key	112

Practice Test *114*

Verbal Skills	114
Mathematics	126
Science	132

Answer Key *140*

Verbal Skills **140**

Mathematics **144**

Science **148**

ONLINE RESOURCES

Trivium includes online resources with the purchase of this study guide to help you fully prepare for the exam.

Practice Test

In addition to the practice test included in this book, we also offer an online exam. Since many exams today are computer based, practicing your test-taking skills on the computer is a great way to prepare.

Review Questions

Need more practice? Our review questions use a variety of formats to help you memorize key terms and concepts.

Flash Cards

Trivium's flash cards allow you to review important terms easily on your computer or smartphone.

Cheat Sheets

Review the core skills you need to master the exam with easy-to-read Cheat Sheets.

From Stress to Success

Watch "From Stress to Success," a brief but insightful YouTube video that offers the tips, tricks, and secrets experts use to score higher on the exam.

Feedback

Let us know what you think!

Access these materials at: ascenciatestprep.com/nex-online-resources

Introduction

What is the NLN-NEX?

The Nursing Entrance Exam (NEX) was developed by the National League of Nursing (NLN) for use by nursing programs during the application process. The exam evaluates candidates' relevant knowledge and skills for placement in nursing education programs.

What's on the NLN-NEX?

The NLN-NEX is a multiple-choice test. It evaluates the test taker's verbal, math, and science skills.

Test	Concepts	Number of Questions	Time
Verbal	reading comprehension (25 questions; 5 passages) word knowledge (25 questions)	50 scored (8 unscored/pretest questions)	60 minutes
Math	numbers and operations (12 questions) measurement (14 questions) algebra (7 questions) data and information (7 questions)	40 scored (5 unscored/pretest questions)	60 minutes
Science	biology (20 questions) chemistry (5 questions) anatomy (11 questions) physiology (11 questions) health (8 questions)	55 scored (5 unscored/pretest questions)	60 minutes
Total		145 scored questions (163 total, including pretest questions)	**3 hours**

How is the NLN-NEX Administered?

The NLN-NEX is a computer-based exam consisting of three tests (described above). It is administered by the National League of Nursing in partnership with nursing schools and programs around the country. To register for an exam, you must create an account with NLN at https://ondemand.questionmark.com/home/405669/user. Once you create an account, you can choose an exam date and location. The exam can be taken remotely (via live, virtual proctoring) or at a test site location.

Before you take the NLN-NEX, carefully check the policies and procedures for your particular test site. Fees and payment methods will vary. In addition, each test site will have specific requirements for what you must bring (e.g., identification, pencils) and what you may not bring (e.g., cell phones). A built-in calculator will be provided for the mathematics portion of the test.

The NLN allows you to retake the NEX; however, each school will have its own policy about which scores they will accept and the time frame during which you may retake the exam. Keep in mind that schools may require you to take the NEX the same year that you are applying.

How is the NLN-NEX Scored?

You will receive a raw score, a composite score, and a percentile score. The raw score will simply show how many questions you answered correctly. The composite score is a weighted, scaled score combining your scores on all of the test sections. It ranges from 0 – 200.

You will receive percentile scores for each section and for the entire test. Percentile scores allow you to compare your performance to that of other candidates. For instance, if you earn a raw score of 55 on Science with a percentile score of 91, that means that 91 percent of other test-takers got raw scores lower than 55 on Science.

Be sure to answer every question on the test. There is no guess penalty; however, questions that remain unanswered will be considered "incorrect."

There is no set "passing" score for the NLN-NEX. Different nursing programs have their own guidelines for how they interpret your scores during the application review process. Contact your school's admissions office to learn more about how they use NLN-NEX score reports.

Ascencia Test Prep

With health care fields such as nursing, pharmacy, emergency care, and physical therapy becoming the fastest-growing industries in the United States, individuals looking to enter the health care industry or rise in their field need high-quality, reliable resources. Ascencia Test Prep's study guides and test preparation materials are developed by credentialed industry professionals with years of experience in their respective fields. Ascencia recognizes that health care professionals nurture bodies and spirits, and save lives. Ascencia Test Prep's mission is to help health care workers grow.

Verbal Skills

The Verbal Skills portion of the NLN-PAX contains sixty reading comprehension and vocabulary questions. This chapter reviews different types of reading comprehension questions and helps you build your vocabulary.

Reading Comprehension

On the NLN-PAX, reading comprehension questions appear as part of the Verbal Ability portion of the exam. There are sixty questions on the Verbal Ability test; approximately forty-eight are reading comprehension questions.

Reading comprehension questions require you to read a short passage. Most passages will be about health or medicine. Each passage is followed by six questions. You do not need any outside knowledge to answer the reading comprehension questions.

This section reviews different types of reading comprehension questions you will encounter.

The Main Idea

The **topic** is a word or short phrase that explains what a passage is about. The **main idea** is a complete sentence that explains what the author is trying to say about the topic. Generally, the **topic sentence** is the first (or near the first) sentence in a paragraph. It is a general statement that introduces the topic so that the reader knows what to expect.

QUICK REVIEW

To find the main idea, identify the topic and then ask, "What is the author trying to tell me about the topic?"

The **summary sentence**, on the other hand, frequently (but not always!) comes at the end of a paragraph or passage because it wraps up all the ideas presented. This sentence summarizes what an author has said about the topic. Some passages, particularly short ones, will not include a summary sentence.

Table 1.1. Identifying Topic and Main Idea	
The cisco, a foot-long freshwater fish native to the Great Lakes, once thrived throughout the basin but had virtually disappeared by the 1950s. However, today fishermen are pulling them up by the netload in Lake Michigan and Lake Ontario. It is highly unusual for a native species to revive, and the reason for the cisco's reemergence is even more unlikely. The cisco have an invasive species—quagga mussels—to thank for their return. Quagga mussels depleted nutrients in the lakes, harming other species highly dependent on these nutrients. Cisco, however, thrive in low-nutrient environments. As other species— many of which were invasive—diminished, cisco flourished in their place.	
Topic sentence	The cisco, a foot-long freshwater fish native to the Great Lakes, once thrived throughout the basin but had virtually disappeared by the 1950s.
Topic	cisco

Table 1.1. Identifying Topic and Main Idea

Summary sentence	As other species—many of which were invasive—diminished, cisco flourished in their place.
Main idea	Cisco had nearly disappeared from the lake, but now flourish thanks to the invasive quagga mussel.

PRACTICE QUESTIONS

1. Tourists flock to Yellowstone National Park each year to view the geysers that bubble and erupt throughout it. What most of these tourists do not know is that these geysers are formed by a caldera—a hot crater in the earth's crust—which was created by a series of three eruptions of an ancient super volcano. These eruptions, which began 2.1 million years ago, spewed between 1,000 to 2,450 cubic kilometers of volcanic matter at such a rate that the volcano's magma chamber collapsed, creating the craters.

What is the topic of the passage?
- A) tourists
- B) geysers
- C) volcanic eruptions
- D) super volcanos

2. The Battle of Little Bighorn, commonly called Custer's Last Stand, was a battle between the Lakota, the Northern Cheyenne, the Arapaho and the Seventh Cavalry Regiment of the US Army. Led by war leaders Crazy Horse and Chief Gall and the religious leader Sitting Bull, the allied tribes of the Plains Indians decisively defeated their US foes. Two hundred and sixty-eight US soldiers were killed, including General George Armstrong Custer, two of his brothers, his nephew, his brother-in-law, and six Indian scouts.

What is the main idea of this passage?
- A) Most of General Custer's family died in the Battle of Little Bighorn.
- B) The Seventh Cavalry regiment was formed to fight Native American tribes.
- C) Sitting Bull and George Custer were fierce enemies.
- D) The Battle of Little Bighorn was a significant victory for the Plains Indians.

Supporting Details

Statements that describe or explain the main idea are **supporting details**. Supporting details are often found after the topic sentence. They support the main idea through examples, descriptions, and explanations.

Authors may add details to support their argument or claim. **Facts** are details that point to truths, while **opinions** are based on personal beliefs or judgments. To differentiate between fact and opinion, look for statements that express feelings, attitudes, or beliefs that can't be proven (opinions) and statements that can be proven (facts).

HELPFUL HINT

To find supporting details, look for sentences that connect to the main idea and tell more about it.

Table 1.2. Supporting Details and Fact and Opinion	
Bait is an important element of fishing. Some people use live bait, such as worms and night crawlers. Others use artificial bait, such as lures and spinners. Live bait has a scent that fish are drawn to. Live bait is a good choice for fishing. It's cheap and easy to find. Lures can vibrate, make noise, and mimic the movements of some fish. People should choose artificial bait over live bait because it can be used multiple times.	
Supporting details	Lures can vibrate, make noise, and mimic the movements of some fish.
Fact	Live bait has a scent that fish are drawn to.
Opinion	Live bait is a good choice for fishing.

PRACTICE QUESTIONS

3. Increasingly, companies are turning to subcontracting services rather than hiring full-time employees. This provides companies with advantages like greater flexibility, reduced legal responsibility to employees, and lower possibility of unionization within the company. However, this has led to increasing confusion and uncertainty over the legal definition of employment. Courts have grappled with questions about the hiring company's responsibility in maintaining fair labor practices. Companies argue that they delegate that authority to subcontractors, while unions and other worker advocate groups argue that companies still have a legal obligation to the workers who contribute to their business.

Which detail BEST supports the idea that contracting employees is beneficial to companies?
 A) Uncertainty over the legal definition of employment increases.
 B) Companies still have a legal obligation to contractors.
 C) There is a lower possibility of unionization within the company.
 D) Contractors, not companies, control fair labor practices.

4. Chalk is a colorful way for kids and adults to have fun and be creative. Chalk is used on playgrounds and sidewalks. Children love to draw pictures in different colors.

The designs are beautiful, but they are also messy. Chalk doesn't clean up easily. It has to wash away. Chalk is also used by cafés and bakeries. Shops use chalk to showcase their menus and special items. It is a great way to advertise their food.

Which statement from the passage is an opinion?
 A) It is a great way to advertise their food.
 B) Chalk doesn't clean up easily.
 C) It has to wash away.
 D) Shops use chalk to showcase their menus and special items.

Drawing Conclusions

Readers can use information that is **explicit**, or clearly stated, along with information that is **implicit**, or indirect, to make inferences and **draw conclusions**. Readers can determine meaning from what is implied by using details, context clues, and prior knowledge. When answering questions, consider what is known from personal experiences and make note of all information the author has provided before drawing a conclusion.

> **HELPFUL HINT**
>
> Look for facts, character actions and dialogue, how each sentence connects to the topic, and the author's reasoning for an argument when drawing conclusions.

Table 1.3. Drawing Conclusions

When the Spanish-American War broke out in 1898, the US Army was small and understaffed. President William McKinley called for 1,250 volunteers to serve in the First US Volunteer Calvary. The ranks were quickly filled by cowboys, gold prospectors, hunters, gamblers, Native Americans, veterans, police officers, and college students looking for an adventure. The officer corps was composed of veterans of previous wars. With more volunteers than it could accept, the army set high standards: all the recruits had to be skilled on horseback and with guns. Consequently, they became known as the Rough Riders.	
Question	Why are the volunteers named Rough Riders?
Explicit information	different people volunteered, men were looking for adventure, recruits had to be extremely skilled on horseback and with guns due to a glut of volunteers
Implicit information	Men had previous occupations, officer corps veterans worked with volunteers.
Conclusion drawn	The men were called Rough Riders because they were inexperienced yet particularly enthusiastic to help with the war and were willing to put in extra effort to join.

PRACTICE QUESTION

5. After World War I, political and social forces pushed for a return to normalcy in the United States. The result was disengagement from the larger world and increased focus on American economic growth and personal enjoyment. Caught in the middle were American writers, raised on the values of the prewar world and frustrated with what they viewed as the superficiality and materialism of postwar American culture. Many of them fled to Paris, where they became known as the "lost generation," creating a trove of literary works criticizing their home culture and delving into their own feelings of alienation.

Which conclusion about the effects of war is most likely true?
- A) War served as an inspiration for literary works.
- B) It was difficult to stabilize countries after war occurred.
- C) Writers were torn between supporting war and their own ideals.
- D) Individual responsibility and global awareness declined after the war.

The Author's Point of View

The **author's purpose** is an author's reason for writing a text. Authors may write to share an experience, entertain, persuade, or inform readers. This can be done through persuasive, expository, and narrative writing.

Persuasive writing influences the actions and thoughts of readers. Authors state an opinion, then provide reasons that support the opinion. **Expository writing** outlines and explains steps in a process. Authors focus on a sequence of events. **Narrative writing** tells a story. Authors include a setting, plot, characters, problem, and solution in the text.

Authors also share their **point of view** (perspectives, attitudes, and beliefs) with readers. Identify the author's point of view by word choice, details, descriptions, and characters' actions. The author's attitude or tone can be found in word choice that conveys feelings or stance on a topic.

Text structure is the way the author organizes a text. A text can be organized to show problem and solution, comparison and contrast, or even cause and effect. Structure of a text can give insight into an author's purpose and point of view. If a text is organized to pose an argument or advertise a product, it can be considered persuasive. The author's point of view will be revealed in how thoughts and opinions are expressed in the text.

> **STUDY TIP**
>
> Use the acronym *P.I.E.S.*—Persuade, Inform, Entertain, State—to help you remember elements of an author's purpose.

Table 1.4. The Author's Purpose and Point of View

Superfoods are foods that are found in nature. They contain rich nutrients and are low in calories. Many people are concerned about healthy diets and weight loss, so superfoods are a great meal choice! Rich antioxidants and vitamins found in superfoods decrease the risk of diseases and aid in heart health.	
Author's purpose	persuade readers of the benefit of superfoods
Point of view	advocates superfoods as "a great meal choice"

Verbal Skills

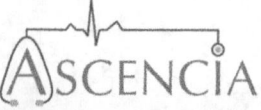

Table 1.4. The Author's Purpose and Point of View	
Tone	positive, encouraging, pointing out the benefits of super-foods, using positive words like great and rich
Structure	cause and effect to show use of superfoods and results

PRACTICE QUESTIONS

6. University of California, Berkeley, researchers decided to tackle an age-old problem: why shoelaces come untied. They recorded the shoelaces of a volunteer walking on a treadmill by attaching devices to record the acceleration, or g-force, experienced by the knot. The results were surprising. A shoelace knot experiences more g-force from a person walking than any rollercoaster can generate. However, if the person simply stomped or swung their feet—the two movements that make up a walker's stride—the g-force was not enough to undo the knots.

What is the purpose of this passage?
    A) to confirm if shoelaces always come undone
    B) to compare the force of treadmills and rollercoasters
    C) to persuade readers to tie their shoes tighter
    D) to describe the results of an experiment on shoelaces

7. What do you do with plastic bottles? Do you throw them away, or do you recycle or reuse them? As landfills continue to fill up, there will eventually be no place to put our trash. If you recycle or reuse bottles, you will help reduce waste and turn something old into a creative masterpiece!

Which of the following BEST describes what the author believes?
    A) Landfills are unnecessary.
    B) Reusing objects requires creativity.
    C) Recycling helps the environment.
    D) Reusing objects is better than recycling.

8. Negative cinematic representations of gorillas have provoked fear and contribute to hunting practices that endanger gorilla populations. It's a shame that many films portray them as scary and aggressive creatures. Their size and features should not be cause for alarm. Gorillas are actually shy and act aggressively only when provoked.

What can be inferred about the author's attitude toward gorillas?
    A) The author is surprised that people do not know the truth about gorillas.
    B) The author is concerned that movies distort people's opinion of gorillas.
    C) The author is saddened by the decrease in gorilla populations.
    D) The author is afraid that gorillas are being provoked.

9. Want smoother skin? Try Face Lace, a mix of shea butter and coconut oil. Like most creams it is soft and easy to apply. We rank #1 in sales and free trials. Our competitor Smooth Moves may be great for blemishes, but we excel at reducing the signs of aging!

What is the structure of this text?
- A) cause and effect
- B) order and sequence
- C) problem and solution
- D) compare and contrast

Comparing Passages

Sometimes readers need to compare and contrast two texts. After reading and identifying the main idea of each text, look for similarities and differences in the main idea, details, claims, evidence, characters, and so on.

HELPFUL HINT

Use a Venn diagram, table, or highlighters to organize similarities and differences between texts.

When answering questions about two texts, first identify whether the question is about a similarity or a difference. Then look for specific details in the text that connect to the answers. After that, determine which answer choice best describes the similarity or difference.

Table 1.5. Comparing Passages	
Apple Cider Vinegar	
Apple cider vinegar has many medicinal properties. It is used for cleaning and disinfecting. When ingested, it lowers blood sugar levels, increasing insulin function and fighting diabetes. Studies are being conducted to determine if it can aid in shrinking tumors and cancer cells, and lower the risk of heart disease.	
Alkaline Water	
Many people believe that alkaline water increases immune system support; prevents cancer; and aids in antiaging, detoxification, and weight loss. Unfortunately, having an excess amount of alkaline water in the body could produce nausea, vomiting, and tremors.	
Similarities (comparison)	Both substances are ingested and used to fight diseases.
Differences (contrast)	Alkaline water has negative side effects, whereas apple cider vinegar is being studied to prove its usefulness.

Verbal Skills

PRACTICE QUESTION

Panda Bears

Panda bears live in China's bamboo forests. They eat bamboo and are excellent tree climbers. New roads and railroads break the flow of the forest, isolating panda populations. This decreases the amount of food pandas can access during the year.

Polar Bears

Polar bears live in the Arctic and are the largest land carnivores in the world. They eat seals and walruses. As the sea gets larger from melting ice, polar bears have to travel longer distances for food. Their thick white fur provides warmth and traction for their feet on the ice. They are good swimmers.

10. Which of these statements BEST compares the information in both texts?
    A) A carnivore's diet depends on animals in the area.
    B) The destruction of habitats affects food supply.
    C) Animals must be able to move easily in their environment.
    D) An animal's population can change its habitat.

Recognizing Sequences

Signal words indicate steps of a process, reveal a sequence of events, or show the **logic** of a passage. These words will tell you when things need to happen in a certain order. Signal words should show a transition from one event or step to another.

When reading a passage, you will find that signal words can be used to follow the direction of the author's ideas and the sequence of events. Signal words show time order and how details flow in a chronological way.

HELPFUL HINT

To find signal words, ask, "What happened first and what happened after that?"

Table 1.6. Following Directions and Recognizing Sequences
NASA wanted to launch a man from Earth to the moon. At first they used satellites for launch tests. Then in June of 1968, astronauts aboard the Apollo 8 launched into space and circled the moon ten times before returning to Earth. Finally, in 1969 three astronauts reached the moon in the Apollo 11 spacecraft. After a successful landing, two members of the crew walked on the moon. During their walk they collected data and samples of rocks. They returned as heroes of space exploration.
Signal words At first, then, finally, after, during

PRACTICE QUESTION

11. Babies learn to move their bodies over time. Head control is first developed at two months to create strong neck, back, and tummy muscles. Next, the abilities to reach, grasp, and sit up with support happen around four to six months. By the end of six months, babies learn to roll over. After six to nine months, babies can sit on their own and crawl. During age nine to twelve months, pulling and standing up are mastered. Finally, after gaining good balance, babies take their first steps!

Which BEST describes the order of a baby's movement over time?
A) roll over, control head, sit up, crawl
B) sit up, roll over, crawl, walk
C) control head, reach, crawl, roll over
D) sit up, grasp, crawl, walk

Vocabulary

The NLN-PAX Verbal Ability test will also ask you to provide definitions or intended meanings of words within sentences. You may have never encountered some of these words before the test, but there are tricks you can use to figure out what they mean.

Context Clues

One of the most fundamental vocabulary skills is using the context in which a word is used to determine its meaning. Your ability to read sentences carefully is extremely useful when it comes to understanding new vocabulary words.

Vocabulary questions on the NLN-PAX often include **sentence context clues** within the sentence that contains the word. There are several clues that can help you understand the context, and therefore the meaning of a word:

Restatement clues state the definition of the word in the sentence. The definition is often set apart from the rest of the sentence by a comma, parentheses, or a colon.

Teachers often prefer teaching students with intrinsic motivation: these students have an internal desire to learn.

Teachers often prefer teaching students with intrinsic motivation: these students have an internal desire to learn.

The meaning of *intrinsic* is restated as *internal*.

Contrast clues include the opposite meaning of a word. Words like *but*, *on the other hand*, and *however* are tip-offs that a sentence contains a contrast clue.

Janet was destitute after she lost her job, but her wealthy sister helped her get back on her feet.

Destitute is contrasted with *wealthy*, so the definition of destitute is "poor."

Positive/negative clues tell you whether a word has a positive or negative meaning.

The film was lauded by critics as stunning, and was nominated for several awards.

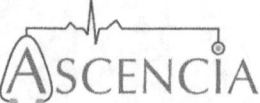

The positive descriptions *stunning* and "nominated for several awards" suggest that *lauded* has a positive meaning.

PRACTICE QUESTIONS

Select the answer that most closely matches the definition of the underlined word as it is used in the sentence.

12. The dog was dauntless in the face of danger, braving the fire to save the girl trapped inside the building.
    A) difficult
    B) fearless
    C) imaginative
    D) startled

13. Beth did not spend any time preparing for the test, but Tyrone kept a rigorous study schedule.
    A) strict
    B) loose
    C) boring
    D) strange

Analyzing Clues

As you know, determining the meaning of a word can be more complicated than just looking in a dictionary. A word might have more than one **denotation**, or definition. The definition the author intends can only be judged by looking at the surrounding text. For example, the word *quack* can refer to the sound a duck makes or to a person who publicly pretends to have a qualification which they do not actually possess.

A word may also have different **connotations**, which are the implied meanings and emotions a word evokes in the reader. For example, a cubicle is simply a walled desk in an office, but for many the word implies a constrictive, uninspiring workplace. Connotations can vary greatly between cultures and even between individuals.

Last, authors might make use of **figurative language**, which is the use of a word to imply something other than the word's literal definition. This is often done by comparing two things. If you say *"I felt like a butterfly when I got a new haircut,"* the listener knows you do not resemble an insect but instead felt beautiful and transformed.

PRACTICE QUESTIONS

Select the answer that most closely matches the definition of the underlined word or phrase as it is used in the sentence.

14. The nurse looked at the patient's eyes and determined from his uneven pupils that brain damage was possible.
    A) part of the eye
    B) young student
    C) walking pace
    D) breathing sounds

15. Aiden examined the antique lamp and worried that he had been taken for a ride. He had paid a lot for the vintage lamp, but it looked like it was worthless.
   A) transported
   B) forgotten
   C) deceived
   D) hindered

Words Structure

You are not expected to know every word in the English language for your test; rather, you will need to use deductive reasoning to find the best definition of the word in question. Many words can be broken down into three main parts to help determine their meaning:

prefix – root – suffix

Roots are the building blocks of all words. Every word is either a root itself or has a root. The root is what is left when you strip away the prefixes and suffixes from a word. For example, in the word *unclear*, if you take away the prefix *un–*, you have the root *clear*.

Roots are not always recognizable words, because they often come from Latin or Greek words, such as *nat*, a Latin root meaning born. The word *native*, which means a person born in a referenced place, comes from this root; so does the word *prenatal*, meaning *before birth*. It is important to keep in mind, however, that roots do not always match the original definitions of words, and they can have several different spellings.

Prefixes are elements added to the beginning of a word, and **suffixes** are elements added to the end of the word; together they are known as **affixes**. They carry assigned meanings and can be attached to a word to completely change the word's meaning or to enhance the word's original meaning.

Let's use the word *prefix* itself as an example: *fix* means to place something securely and *pre–* means before. Therefore, *prefix* means to place something before or in front of. Now let's look at a suffix: in the word *feminism*, *femin* is a root which means female. The suffix *–ism* means act, practice, or process. Thus, *feminism* is the process of establishing equal rights for women.

Although you cannot determine the meaning of a word from a prefix or suffix alone, you can use this knowledge to eliminate answer choices. Understanding whether the word is positive or negative can give you the partial meaning of the word.

> **QUICK REVIEW**
>
> Can you figure out the definitions of the following words using their parts?
>
> - ambidextrous
> - anthropology
> - diagram
> - egocentric
> - hemisphere
> - homicide
> - metamorphosis
> - nonsense
> - portable
> - rewind
> - submarine
> - triangle
> - unicycle

Table 1.7. Common Roots

Root	Definition	Example
ast(er)	star	asteroid, astronomy
audi	hear	audience, audible
auto	self	automatic, autograph
bene	good	beneficent, benign
bio	life	biology, biorhythm
cap	take	capture
ced	yield	secede
chrono	time	chronometer, chronic
corp	body	corporeal
crac or crat	rule	autocrat
demo	people	democracy
dict	say	dictionary, dictation
duc	lead or make	ductile, produce
gen	give birth	generation, genetics
geo	earth	geography, geometry
grad	step	graduate
graph	write	graphical, autograph
ject	throw	eject
jur or jus	law	justice, jurisdiction
juven	young	juvenile
log or logue	thought	logic, logarithm
luc	light	lucidity
man	hand	manual
mand	order	remand
mis	send	transmission
mono	one	monotone
omni	all	omnivore
path	feel	sympathy
phil	love	philanthropy

Table 1.7. Common Roots		
Root	Definition	Example
phon	sound	phonograph
port	carry	export
qui	rest	quiet
scrib or script	write	scribe, transcript
sense or sent	feel	sentiment
tele	far away	telephone
terr	earth	terrace
uni	single	unicode
vac	empty	vacant
vid or vis	see	video, vision

PRACTICE QUESTIONS

Select the answer that most closely matches the definition of the underlined word as it is used in the sentence.

16. The bellicose dog will be sent to training school next week.
    A) misbehaved
    B) friendly
    C) scared
    D) aggressive

17. The new menu rejuvenated the restaurant and made it one of the most popular spots in town.
    A) established
    B) invigorated
    C) improved
    D) motivated

Answer Key

1. B: The topic of the passage is geysers. Tourists, volcanic eruptions, and super volcanos are all mentioned in the explanation of what geysers are and how they are formed.

2. D: The author writes that "the allied tribes...decisively defeated their US foes," and the remainder of the passage provides details to support this idea.

3. C: The passage specifically presents this detail as one of the advantages of subcontracting services.

4. A: The statement "It is a great way to advertise their food" is a judgment about how the shops use chalk to show menu items to customers. The word *great* expresses a feeling, and the idea cannot be proven.

5. D: After the war, there was a lack of focus on the world and greater focus on personal comforts, which writers viewed as superficiality and materialism.

6. D: The text provides details on the experiment as well as its results.

7. C: The author states that recycling and reusing objects reduces waste, which helps the environment.

8. B: The author demonstrates disapproval of film portrayals of gorillas and how they influence people's views of gorillas.

9. D: In this text, two brands of cream are being compared and contrasted.

10. B: Both passages indicate that habitats are diminishing, impacting access to food.

11. B: According to the passage, a baby achieves milestones in independent movement in this order. Use the ages and signal words to determine the order of events.

12. B: Demonstrating bravery in the face of danger would be *fearless*. The restatement clue (*braving*) tells you exactly what the word means.

13. A: The word *but* tells us that Tyrone studied in a different way than Beth, which means it is a contrast clue. If Beth did not study hard, then Tyrone did. The best answer, therefore, is choice A.

14. A: Only choice A matches both the definition of the word and context of the sentence. Choice B is an alternative definition for pupil, but does not make sense in the sentence. Both C and D could be correct in the context of the sentence, but neither is a definition of pupil.

15. C: It is clear from the context of the sentence that Aiden was not literally taken for a ride. Instead, this phrase is an example of figurative language. From context clues you can figure out that Aiden paid too much for the lamp, so he was deceived.

16. D: The prefix *belli*–, which means "warlike," can be used to confirm that "aggressive" is the right answer.

17. B: All the answer choices could make sense in the context of the sentence, so it is necessary to use word structure to find the definition. The root *juven* means young and the prefix *re*– means again, so *rejuvenate* means to be made young again. The answer choice with the most similar meaning is *invigorated*, which means to give something energy.

Mathematics

Types of Numbers

Numbers are placed in categories based on their properties.

A **natural number** is greater than zero and has no decimal or fraction attached. These are also sometimes called counting numbers. {1,2,3,4,...}

Whole numbers are natural numbers and the number zero. {0,1,2,3,4,...}

Integers include positive and negative natural numbers and zero. {...,−4,−3,−2,−1,0,1,2,3,4,...}

A **rational number** can be represented as a fraction. Any decimal part must terminate or resolve into a repeating pattern. Examples include -12, $-\frac{4}{2}$, 0.36, 7.7, $26\frac{1}{5}$, etc.

An **irrational number** cannot be represented as a fraction. An irrational decimal number never ends and never resolves into a repeating pattern. Examples include $-\sqrt{7}$, π, and 0.34567989135 ...

A **real number** is a number that can be represented by a point on a number line. Real numbers include all the rational and irrational numbers.

> **HELPFUL HINT**
>
> If a real number is a natural number (e.g. 50), then it is also an integer, a whole number, and a rational number.

Every natural number (except 1) is either a prime number or a composite number. A **prime number** is a natural number greater than 1 which can only be divided evenly by 1 and itself. For example, 7 is a prime number because it can only be divided by the numbers 1 and 7.

On the other hand, a **composite number** is a natural number greater than 1 which can be evenly divided by at least one other number besides 1 and itself. For example, 6 is a composite number because it can be divided by 1, 2, 3, and 6.

Composite numbers can be broken down into prime numbers using factor trees. For example, the number 54 is 2×27, and 27 is 3×9, and 9 is 3×3, as shown in Figure 2.1.

Once the number has been broken down into its simplest form, the composite number can be expressed as a product of prime factors. Repeated factors can be written using exponents. An **exponent** shows how many times a number should be multiplied by itself. As shown in the factor tree, the number 54 can be written as $2 \times 3 \times 3 \times 3$ or 2×3^3.

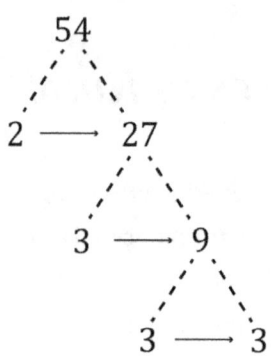

PRACTICE QUESTIONS

Classify the following numbers as natural, whole, integer, rational, or irrational. (The numbers may have more than one classification.)

1. 72
2. $-\frac{2}{3}$
3. $\sqrt{5}$

Scientific Notation

Scientific notation is a method of representing very large and small numbers in the form $a \times 10^n$ where a is a value between 1 and 10, and n is an integer. For example, the number 927,000,000 is written in scientific notation as 9.27×10^8. Multiplying 9.27 by 10 eight times gives 927,000,000. When performing operations with scientific notation, the final answer should be in the form $a \times 10^n$.

Table 2.1. Place Value									
1,000,000	100,000	10,000	1,000	100	10	1	.	$\frac{1}{10}$	$\frac{1}{100}$
10^6	10^5	10^4	10^3	10^2	10^1	10^0		10^{-1}	10^{-2}
Millions	Hundred Thousands	Ten Thousands	Thousands	Hundreds	Tens	Ones	Decimal	Tenths	Hundredths

When adding and subtracting numbers in scientific notation, the power of 10 must be the same for all numbers. This results in like terms in which the a terms are added or subtracted and the 10^n remains unchanged. When multiplying numbers in scientific notation, multiply the a factors and add the exponents. For division, divide the a factors and subtract the exponents.

PRACTICE QUESTIONS

4. Simplify: $(3.8 \times 10^3) + (4.7 \times 10^2)$

5. Simplify: $(8.1 \times 10^{-5})(1.4 \times 10^7)$

Positive and Negative Numbers

Positive numbers are greater than zero, and **negative numbers** are less than zero. Both positive and negative numbers can be shown on a **number line**.

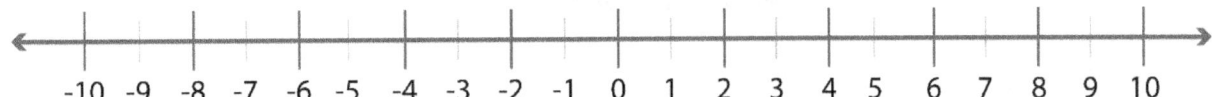

Positive and negative numbers can be added, subtracted, multiplied, and divided. The sign of the resulting number is governed by a specific set of rules shown in the table below.

Table 2.2. Operations with Positive and Negative Numbers	
Adding Real Numbers	
Positive + Positive = Positive	$7 + 8 = 15$
Negative + Negative = Negative	$-7 + (-8) = -15$
Negative + Positive = Keep the sign of the number with the larger absolute value	$-7 + 8 = 1$ $7 + (-8) = -1$
Subtracting Real Numbers	
Change the subtraction to addition, change the sign of the second number, and use addition rules.	
Negative − Positive = Negative	$-7 - 8 = -7 + (-8) = -15$
Positive − Negative = Positive	$7 - (-8) = 7 + 8 = 15$
Negative − Negative = Keep the sign of the number with the larger absolute value.	$-7 - (-8) = -7 + 8 = 1$ $-8 - (-7) = -8 + 7 = -1$
Positive − Positive = Positive if the first number is larger Negative if the second number is larger	$8 - 4 = 4$ $4 - 8 = -4$
Multiplying Real Numbers	
Positive × Positive = Positive	$8 \times 4 = 32$
Negative × Negative = Positive	$-8 \times (-4) = 32$
Negative × Positive = Negative	$8 \times (-4) = -32$ $-8 \times 4 = -32$
Dividing Real Numbers	

Mathematics

Table 2.2. Operations with Positive and Negative Numbers	
Positive ÷ Positive = Positive	$8 \div 4 = 2$
Negative ÷ Negative = Positive	$-8 \div (-4) = 2$
Positive ÷ Negative OR Negative ÷ Positive = Negative	$8 \div (-4) = -2$ $-8 \div 4 = -2$

PRACTICE QUESTIONS

Add or subtract the following real numbers:

6. $-18 + 12$

7. $-3.64 + (-2.18)$

8. $9.37 - 4.25$

9. $86 - (-20)$

Multiply or divide the following real numbers:

10. $\frac{10}{3} - \frac{9}{5}$

11. $\frac{-64}{-10}$

12. $(2.2)(3.3)$

Order of Operations

When solving a multi-step equation, the **order of operations** must be used to get the correct answer. Generally speaking, the problem should be worked in the following order: 1) parentheses and brackets; 2) exponents and square roots; 3) multiplication and division; 4) addition and subtraction. The acronym PEMDAS can be used to remember the order of operations.

Please **E**xcuse (**M**y **D**ear) (**A**unt **S**ally)

P — Parentheses: Calculate expressions inside parentheses, brackets, braces, etc.

E — Exponents: Calculate exponents and square roots.

M — Multiply and **D** — Divide: Calculate any remaining multiplication and division in order from left to right.

A — Add and **S** — Subtract: Calculate any remaining addition and subtraction in order from left to right.

The steps "Multiply-Divide" and "Addition-Subtraction" go in order from left to right. In other words, divide before multiplying if the division problem is on the left.

For example, the expression $(3^2 - 2)^2 + (4)5^3$ is simplified using the following steps:

Parentheses: Because the parentheses in this problem contain two operations (exponents and subtraction), use the order of operations within the parentheses. Exponents come before subtraction.

$$(3^2 - 2)^2 + (4)5^3 = (9 - 2)^2 + (4)5^3 = (7)^2 + (4)5^3$$

- Exponents: $(7)^2 + (4)5^3 = 49 + (4)125$
- Multiplication and division: $49 + (4)125 = 49 + 500$
- Addition and subtraction: $49 + 500 = 549$

PRACTICE QUESTIONS

14. Simplify: $2(21 - 14) + 6 \div (-2) \times 3 - 10$

15. Simplify: $-3^2 + 4(5) + (5 - 6)^2 - 8$

16. Simplify: $\frac{(7-9)^3 + 8(10-12)}{4^2 - 5^2}$

Decimals and Fractions

Decimals

A **decimal** is a number that contains a decimal point. The place value for a decimal includes **tenths** (one place after the decimal point), **hundredths** (two places after the decimal point), **thousandths** (three places after the decimal point), etc.

5	4	.	3	2
5×10^1	4×10^0	Decimal Point	3×10^{-1}	2×10^{-2}
5×10	4×1		$3 \times 1 \over 10$	$2 \times 1 \over 100$
50	4		0.3	0.02
$50 + 4 + 0.3 + 0.02 = 54.32$					

Figure 2.3. Decimals and Place Value

Decimals can be added, subtracted, multiplied, and divided:

To add or subtract decimals, line up the decimal points and perform the operation, keeping the decimal point in the same place in the answer.

```
  12.35
+  3.63
= 15.98
```

HELPFUL HINT

If you're unsure which way to move the decimal after multiplying, remember that changing the decimal should always make the final answer smaller.

To multiply decimals, first multiply the numbers without the decimal points. Then, add the number of decimal places to the right of the decimal point in the original numbers and place the decimal point in the answer so that there are that many places to the right of the decimal.

$$12.35 \times 3.63 =$$

$$1{,}235 \times 363 = 448{,}305 \rightarrow 44.8305$$

When dividing decimals, move the decimal point to the right in order to make the divisor a whole number and move the decimal the same number of places in the dividend. Divide the numbers without regard to the decimal. Then, place the decimal point of the quotient directly above the decimal point of the dividend.

$$\frac{12.35}{3.63} = \frac{1{,}235}{363} = 3.4$$

PRACTICE QUESTIONS

17. Simplify: $24.38 + 16.51 - 29.87$

18. Simplify: $(10.4)(18.2)$

19. Simplify: $80 \div 2.5$

Fractions

A **fraction** is a number that can be written in the form $\frac{a}{b}$ where b is not equal to zero.

The a part of the fraction is the numerator (top number) and b part of the fraction is the denominator (bottom number).

If the denominator of a fraction is greater than the numerator, the value of the fraction is less than 1 and it is called a **proper fraction** (e.g., $\frac{3}{5}$ is a proper fraction).

In an **improper fraction**, the denominator is less than the numerator and the value of the fraction is greater than one (e.g. $\frac{8}{3}$ is an improper fraction). An improper fraction can be written as a whole number or a mixed number. A **mixed number** has a whole number part and a proper fraction part. Improper fractions can be converted to mixed numbers by dividing the numerator by the denominator, which gives the whole number part, and the remainder becomes the numerator of the proper fraction part (for example: improper fraction $\frac{25}{9}$ is equal to mixed number $2\frac{7}{9}$ because 9 divides into 25 two times, with a remainder of 7).

Conversely, mixed numbers can be converted to improper fractions. To do so, determine the numerator of the improper fraction by multiplying the denominator by the whole number, then adding the numerator. The final number is written as the (now larger) numerator over the original denominator.

HELPFUL HINT

$$a\frac{m}{n} = \frac{n \times a \times m}{n}$$

Fractions with the same denominator can be added or subtracted by simply adding or subtracting the numerators; the denominator will remain unchanged.
If the fractions to be added or subtracted do not have a common denominator, the least common multiple of the denominators must be found. The quickest way to find a common denominator of a set of values is simply to multiply all the values together. The result might not be the least common denominator, but it will get the job done.

In the operation $\frac{2}{3} - \frac{1}{2}$, the common denominator will be a multiple of both 3 and 2.

Multiples are found by multiplying the denominator by whole numbers until a common multiple is found:

multiples of 3 are **3** (3×1), **6** (3×2), **9** (3×3) ...

multiples of 2 are **2** (2×1), **4** (2×2), **6** (2×3) ...

Since 6 is the smallest multiple of both 3 and 2, it is the least common multiple and can be used as the common denominator. Both the numerator and denominator of each fraction should be multiplied by the appropriate whole number:

$$\left(\frac{2}{3}\right)\left(\frac{2}{2}\right) - \left(\frac{1}{2}\right)\left(\frac{3}{3}\right) = \frac{4}{6} - \frac{3}{6} = \frac{1}{6}$$

When multiplying fractions, simply multiply each numerator together and each denominator together, reducing the result if possible. To divide two fractions, invert the second fraction (swap the numerator and denominator), then multiply normally. If there are any mixed numbers when multiplying or dividing, they should first be changed to improper fractions. Note that multiplying proper fractions creates a value smaller than either original value.

$$\frac{5}{6} \times \frac{2}{3} = \frac{10}{18} = \frac{5}{9}$$

$$\frac{5}{6} \div \frac{2}{3} = \frac{5}{6} \times \frac{3}{2} = \frac{15}{12} = \frac{5}{4}$$

PRACTICE QUESTIONS

20. Simplify: $2\frac{3}{5} + 3\frac{1}{4} - 1\frac{1}{2}$

21. Simplify: $\frac{7}{8}\left(3\frac{1}{3}\right)$

22. Simplify: $4\frac{1}{2} \div \frac{2}{3}$

Converting Between Fractions and Decimals

A fraction is converted to a decimal by using long division until there is no remainder or a pattern of repeating numbers occurs.

$$\frac{1}{2} = 1 \div 2 = 0.5$$

To convert a decimal to a fraction, place the numbers to the right of the decimal over the appropriate base-10 power and simplify the fraction.

$$0.375 = \frac{375}{1,000} = \frac{3}{8}$$

PRACTICE QUESTIONS

23. Write the fraction $\frac{7}{8}$ as a decimal.

24. Write the fraction $\frac{5}{11}$ as a decimal.

25. Write the decimal 0.125 as a fraction.

Rounding and Estimation

Rounding is a way of simplifying a complicated number. The result of rounding will be a less precise value that is easier to write or perform operations on. Rounding is performed to a specific place value, such as the thousands or tenths place.

The rules for rounding are as follows:

- Underline the place value being rounded to.
- Locate the digit one place value to the right of the underlined value. If this value is less than 5, keep the underlined value and replace all digits to the right of the underlined value with zero. If the value to the right of the underlined digit is more than 5, increase the underlined digit by one and replace all digits to the right of it with zero.

HELPFUL HINT

Estimation can often be used to eliminate answer choices on multiple choice tests without having to completely work the problem.

Estimation is when numbers are rounded and then an operation is performed. This process can be used when working with large numbers to find a close, but not exact, answer.

PRACTICE QUESTIONS

26. Round the number 138,472 to the nearest thousand.

27. The populations of five local towns are 12,341, 8,975, 9,431, 10,521, and 11,427. Estimate the population to the nearest 1,000 people.

Ratios

A **ratio** is a comparison of two numbers and can be represented as $\frac{a}{b}$ ($b \neq 0$), a:b, or a to b. The two numbers represent a constant relationship, not a specific value: for every a number of items in the first group, there will be b number of items in the second. For example, if the ratio of blue to red candies in a bag is 3:5, the bag will contain 3 blue candies for every 5 red candies. So the bag might contain 3 blue candies and 5 red candies, or it might contain 30 blue candies and 50 red candies, or 36 blue candies and 60 red candies. All of these values are representative of the ratio 3:5 (which is the ratio in its lowest, or simplest, terms).

To find the "whole" when working with ratios, simply add the values in the ratio. For example, if the ratio of boys to girls in a class is 2 : 3, the "whole" is five: 2 out of every 5 students are boys, and 3 out of every 5 students are girls.

PRACTICE QUESTIONS

28. There are 10 boys and 12 girls in a first-grade class. What is the ratio of boys to the total number of students? What is the ratio of girls to boys?

28. A family spends $600 a month on rent, $400 on utilities, $750 on groceries, and $550 on miscellaneous expenses. What is the ratio of the family's rent to their total expenses?

Proportions

A **proportion** is an equation which states that two ratios are equal. Proportions are given in the form $\frac{a}{b} = \frac{c}{d}$, where the a and d terms are the extremes and the b and c terms are the means. A proportion is solved using **cross-multiplication** to create an equation with no fractional components:

$$\frac{a}{b} = \frac{c}{d} \rightarrow ad = bc$$

PRACTICE QUESTIONS

30. Solve the proportion for x: $\frac{3-5x}{2} = \frac{-8}{3}$

31. A map is drawn such that 2.5 inches on the map equates to an actual distance of 40 miles. If the distance between two cities measured on the map is 17.25 inches, what is the actual distance between them in miles?

32. At a certain factory, every 4 out of 1,000 parts made will be defective. If in a month there are 125,000 parts made, how many of these parts will be defective?

Percentages

A **percent** (or percentage) means per hundred and is expressed with a percent symbol (%). For example, 54% means 54 out of every 100. A percent can be converted to a decimal by removing the % symbol and moving the decimal point two places to the left, while a decimal can be converted to a percent by moving the decimal point two places to the right and attaching the % sign.

A percent can be converted to a fraction by writing the percent as a fraction with 100 as the denominator and reducing. A fraction can be converted to a percent by performing the indicated division, multiplying the result by 100 and attaching the % sign.

The percent equation has three variables: the part, the whole, and the percent (which is expressed in the equation as a decimal). The equation, as shown below, can be rearranged to solve for any of these variables.

$$\text{part} = \text{whole} \times \text{percent}$$

Mathematics

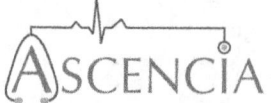

$$\text{percent} = \frac{\text{part}}{\text{whole}}$$

$$\text{whole} = \frac{\text{part}}{\text{percent}}$$

This set of equations can be used to solve percent word problems. All that is needed is to identify the part, whole, and/or percent, then to plug those values into the appropriate equation and solve.

PRACTICE QUESTIONS

33. Write 18% as a fraction.

34. Write $\frac{3}{5}$ as a percent.

35. Write 1.125 as a percent.

36. Write 84% as a decimal.

37. In a school of 650 students, 54% of the students are boys. How many students are girls?

Percent Change

Percent change problems involve a change from an original amount. Often percent change problems appear as word problems that include discounts, growth, or markups. In order to solve percent change problems, it is necessary to identify the percent change (as a decimal), the amount of change, and the original amount. (Keep in mind that one of these will be the value being solved for.) These values can then be plugged into the equations below:

$$\text{amount of change} = \text{original amount} \times \text{percent change}$$

$$\text{percent change} = \frac{\text{amount of change}}{\text{original amount}}$$

$$\text{original amount} = \frac{\text{amount of change}}{\text{percent change}}$$

PRACTICE QUESTIONS

38. A Smart HDTV that originally cost $1,500 is on sale for 45% off. What is the sale price for the item?

39. A house was purchased in 2000 for $100,000 and sold in 2015 for $120,000. What was the percent growth in the value of the house from 2000 to 2015?

Comparison of Rational Numbers

Rational numbers can be ordered from least to greatest (or greatest to least) by placing them in the order in which they fall on a number line. When comparing a set of fractions, it is often easiest to convert each value to a common denominator. Then, it is only necessary to compare the numerators of each fraction.

HELPFUL HINT

Drawing a number line can help when comparing numbers: the final list should go in order from left to right (least to greatest) or right to left (greatest to least) on the line.

When working with numbers in multiple forms (for example, a group of fractions and decimals), convert the values so that the set contains only fractions or only decimals. When ordering negative numbers, remember that the negative number with the largest absolute value is furthest from 0 and is therefore the smallest number. (For example, −75 is smaller than −25.)

PRACTICE QUESTIONS

40. Order the following numbers from greatest to least: $-\frac{2}{3}, 1.2, 0, -2.1, \frac{5}{4}, -1, \frac{1}{8}$.

41. Order the following numbers from least to greatest: $\frac{1}{3}, -\frac{5}{6}, 1\frac{1}{8}, \frac{7}{12}, -\frac{3}{4}, -\frac{3}{2}$.

Algebraic Expressions

The foundation of algebra is the **variable**, an unknown number represented by a symbol (usually a letter such as x or a). Variables can be preceded by a **coefficient**, which is a constant (i.e., a real number) in front of the variable, such as $4x$ or $-2a$. An **algebraic expression** is any sum, difference, product, or quotient of variables and numbers (for example $3x^2$, $2x + 7y - 1$, and $\frac{5}{x}$ are algebraic expressions). **Terms** are any quantities that are added or subtracted (for example, the terms of the expression $x^2 - 3x + 5$ are $x^2, 3x$, and 5). A **polynomial expression** is an algebraic expression where all the exponents on the variables are whole numbers. A polynomial with two terms is known as a **binomial**, and one with three terms is a **trinomial**.

Mathematics

PRACTICE QUESTION

42. If $m = 4$, find the value of the following expression: $5(m-2)^3 + 3m^2 - \frac{m}{4} - 1$

Operations with Expressions

Adding and Subtracting

Expressions can be added or subtracted by simply adding and subtracting **like terms**, which are terms with the same variable part (the variables must be the same, with the same exponents on each variable). For example, in the expressions $2x + 3xy - 2z$ and $6y + 2xy$, the like terms are $3xy$ and $2xy$. Adding the two expressions yields the new expression $2x + 5xy - 2z + 6y$. Note that the other terms did not change; they cannot combine because they have different variables.

PRACTICE QUESTION

43. If $a = 12x + 7xy - 9y$ and $b = 8x - 9xz + 7z$, what is $a + b$?

Distributing and Factoring

Often, simplifying expressions requires distributing and factoring, which can be seen as two sides of the same coin. **Distribution** multiplies each term in the first factor by each term in the second factor to clear off parentheses, while **factoring** reverses this process, taking a polynomial in standard form and writing it as a product of two or more factors.

When distributing a monomial through a polynomial, the expression outside the parentheses is multiplied by each term inside the parentheses. Remember, coefficients are multiplied and exponents are added, following the rules of exponents.

> **HELPFUL HINT**
>
> Operations with polynomials can always be checked by plugging the same value into both expressions.

The first step in factoring a polynomial is always to "undistribute," or factor out, the greatest common factor (GCF) among the terms. The GCF is multiplied by, in parentheses, the expression that remains of each term when the GCF is divided out of each term. Factoring can be checked by multiplying the GCF factor through the parentheses again.

PRACTICE QUESTIONS

44. Expand the following expression: $5x(x^2 - 2c + 10)$

45. Expand the following expression: $x(5 + z) - z(4x - z^2)$

Linear Equations

An **equation** states that two expressions are equal to each other. Polynomial equations are categorized by the highest power of the variables they contain. For instance, the highest power of any exponent of a linear equation is 1, a quadratic equation has a variable raised to the second power, a cubic equation has a variable raised to the third power, and so on.

Solving Linear Equations

Solving an equation means finding the value(s) of the variable that make the equation true. To solve a linear equation, it is necessary to manipulate the terms so that the variable being solved for appears alone on exactly one side of the equal sign while everything else in the equation is on the other side.

The way to solve linear equations is to "undo" all the operations that connect numbers to the variable of interest. Follow these steps:

1. Eliminate fractions by multiplying each side by the least common multiple of any denominators.

2. Distribute to eliminate parentheses, braces, and brackets.

3. Combine like terms.

4. Use addition or subtraction to collect all terms containing the variable of interest to one side, and all terms not containing the variable to the other side.

5. Use multiplication or division to remove coefficients from the variable being solved for.

> **HELPFUL HINT**
>
> On multiple-choice tests, you can avoid solving equations by just plugging the answer choices into the given equation to see which value makes the equation true.

Sometimes there are no numeric values in the equation, or there will be a mix of numerous variables and constants. The goal will be to solve the equation for one of the variables in terms of the other variables. In this case, the answer will be an expression involving numbers and letters instead of a numeric value.

PRACTICE QUESTIONS

46. Solve for x: $100(x + 5) = 1$.

47. Solve for x: $2(x + 2)^2 - 2x^2 + 10 = 20$

Graphs of Linear Equations

The most common way to write a linear equation is **slope-intercept form**:

Mathematics

$$y = mx + b$$

In this equation, m is the **slope**, and b is the **y-intercept**. Slope is often described as "rise over run" because it is calculated as the difference in y-values (rise) over the difference in x-values (run). The slope of the line is also the **rate of change** of the dependent variable y with respect to the independent variable x. The y-intercept is the point where the line crosses the y-axis, or where x equals zero.

> **HELPFUL HINT**
>
> Use the phrase **begin, move** to remember that b is the $y-$intercept (where to begin) and m is the slope (how the line moves).

To graph a linear equation, identify the y-intercept and place that point on the y-axis. Then, starting at the y-intercept, use the slope to count up (or down if negative) the "rise" part of the slope and to the right the "run" part of the slope to find a second point. These points can then be connected to draw the line. To find the equation of a line, identify the y-intercept, if possible, on the graph and use two easily identifiable points to find the slope.

PRACTICE QUESTIONS

48. What is the equation of the following line?

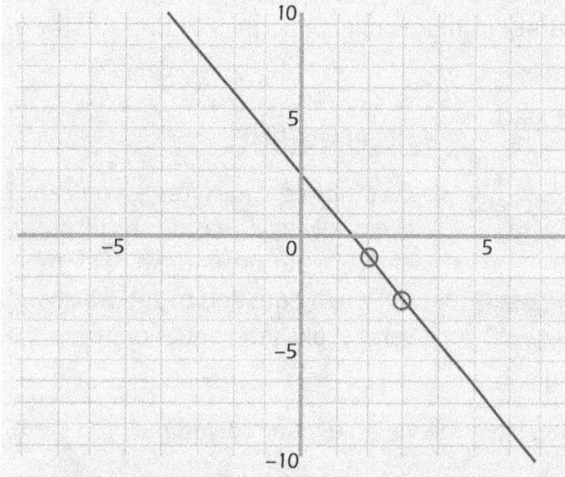

49. What is the slope of the line whose equation is $6x - 2y - 8 = 0$?

Building Equations

In word problems, it is often necessary to translate a verbal description of a relationship into a mathematical equation. No matter the problem, this process can be done using the same steps:

1. Read the problem carefully and identify what value needs to be solved for.

2. Identify the known and unknown quantities in the problem, and assign the unknown quantities a variable.

3. Create equations using the variables and known quantities.

4. Solve the equations.

5. Check the solution: Does it answer the question asked in the problem? Does it make sense?

PRACTICE QUESTIONS

50. A school is holding a raffle to raise money. There is a $3.00 entry fee, and each ticket costs $5.00. If a student paid $28.00, how many tickets did he buy?

51. Abby needs $395 to buy a new bicycle. She has borrowed $150 from her parents, and plans to earn the rest of the money working as a waitress. If she makes $10 per hour, how many hours will she need to work to pay for her new bicycle?

Inequalities

Inequalities are similar to equations, but both sides of the problem are not equal (≠). Inequalities may be represented as follows: greater than (>), greater than or equal to (≥), less than (<), or less than or equal to (≤). For example, the statement "12 is less than 4 times x" would be written as 12<4x.

Inequalities can be solved by manipulating them much like equations. However, the solution to an inequality is a set of numbers, not a single value. For example, simplifying $4x + 2 \leq 14$ gives the inequality $x \leq 3$, meaning every number less than 3 would also be included in the set of correct answers.

> **HELPFUL HINT**
>
> Use the acronym **STAR** to remember word problem strategies. Search the problem, Translate into an expression or equation, Answer, and Review.

PRACTICE QUESTIONS

52. Solve the inequality: $4x + 10 > 58$

53. The students on the track team are buying new uniforms. T-shirts cost $12, pants cost $15, and a pair of shoes costs $45. If they have a budget of $2,500, write a mathematical sentence that represents how many of each item they can buy.

Units of Measurement

The standard units for the metric and American systems are shown below along with the prefixes used to express metric units.

Table 2.3. American and SI Units		
Dimension	**American**	**SI**
Length	inch/foot/yard/mile	meter
Mass	ounce/pound/ton	gram
Volume	cup/pint/quart/gallon	liter
Force	pound-force	newton
Pressure	pound-force per square inch	pascal
Work and energy	cal/British thermal unit	joule
Temperature	Fahrenheit	kelvin
Charge	faraday	coulomb

Table 2.4. Metric Prefixes		
Prefix	**Symbol**	**Multiplication Factor**
tera	T	1,000,000,000,000
giga	G	1,000,000,000
mega	M	1,000,000
kilo	k	1,000
hecto	h	100
deca	da	10
base unit	--	--
deci	d	0.1
centi	c	0.01
milli	m	0.001
micro	μ	0.000001
nano	n	0.000000001
pico	p	0.000000000001

Table 2.5. Conversion Factors	
1 in. = 2.54 cm	1 lb. = 0.454 kg
1 yd. = 0.914 m	1 cal = 4.19 J
1 mi. = 1.61 km	$1°F = \frac{9}{5}°C + 32°C$
1 gal. = 3.785 L	$1 \text{ cm}^3 = 1 \text{ mL}$
1 oz. = 28.35 g	1 hr = 3,600 s

HELPFUL HINT

A mnemonic device to help remember the metric system between kilo- and milli- is King Henry Drinks Under Dark Chocolate Moon (KHDUDCM).

Units can be converted within a single system or between systems. When converting from one unit to another unit, a **conversion factor** (a fraction used to convert a value with a unit into another unit) is used. For example, there are 2.54 centimeters in 1 inch, so the conversion factor from inches to centimeters is $\frac{2.54 \text{ centimeters}}{1 \text{ inch}}$.

To convert between units, multiply the original value by a conversion factor (or several if needed) so that the original units cancel, leaving the desired unit. Remember that the original value can be made into a fraction by placing it over 1.

$$3 \text{ inches} \times \frac{2.54 \text{ centimeters}}{1 \text{ inch}} = 7.62 \text{ centimeters}$$

Units can be canceled (meaning they disappear from the expression) when they appear on the top and the bottom of a fraction. If the same unit appears in the top (or bottom) of both fractions, you probably need to flip the conversion factor.

PRACTICE QUESTIONS

54. Convert 4.25 kilometers to meters.

55. Convert 12 feet to inches.

Statistics

Statistics is the study of data. Analyzing data requires using **measures of central tendency** (mean, median, and mode) to identify trends or patterns.

The **mean** is the average; it is determined by adding all outcomes and then dividing by the total number of outcomes. For example, the average of the data set

HELPFUL HINT

Mode is most common. Median is in the middle (like a median in the road). Mean is average.

$\{16, 19, 19, 25, 27, 29, 75\}$ is equal to $\frac{16+19+19+25+27+29+75}{7} = \frac{210}{7} = 30$.

Mathematics

The **median** is the number in the middle when the data set is arranged in order from least to greatest. For example, in the data set {16,19,19,25,27,29,75}, the median is 25. When a data set contains an even number of values, finding the median requires averaging the two middle values. In the data set {75,80,82,100}, the two numbers in the middle are 80 and 82. Consequently, the median will be the average of these two values: (80+82)/2=81.

Finally, the **mode** is the most frequent outcome in a data set. In the set {16, 19, 19, 25, 27, 29, 75}, the mode is 19 because it occurs twice, which is more than any of the other numbers. If several values appear an equal, and most frequent, number of times, both values are considered the mode. If every value in a data set appears only once, the data set has no mode.

Other useful indicators include range and outliers. The **range** is the difference between the highest and the lowest values in a data set. For example, the range of the set {16, 19, 19, 25, 27, 29, 75} is $75 - 16 = 59$.

Outliers, or data points that are much different from other data points, should be noted as they can skew the central tendency. In the data set {16, 19, 19, 25, 27, 29, 75}, the value 75 is far outside the other values and raises the value of the mean. Without the outlier, the mean is much closer to the other data points.

$$\frac{16+19+19+25+27+29+75}{7} = \frac{210}{7} = 30$$

$$\frac{16+19+19+25+27+29}{6} = \frac{135}{6} = 22.5$$

Generally, the median is a better indicator of a central tendency if outliers are present to skew the mean.

Trends in a data set can also be seen by graphing the data as a dot plot. The distribution of the data can then be described based on the shape of the graph. A **symmetric** distribution looks like two mirrored halves, while a **skewed** distribution is weighted more heavily toward the right or the left. Note the direction of the skew describes the side of the graph with fewer data points. In a **uniform** data set, the points are distributed evenly along the graph.

A symmetric or skewed distribution may have peaks, or sets of data points that appear more frequently. A **unimodal** distribution has one peak while a **bimodal** distribution has two peaks. A normal (or bell-shaped) distribution is a special symmetric, unimodal graph with a specific distribution of data points.

Practice Questions

58. Which of the following best describes the distribution of the graph?

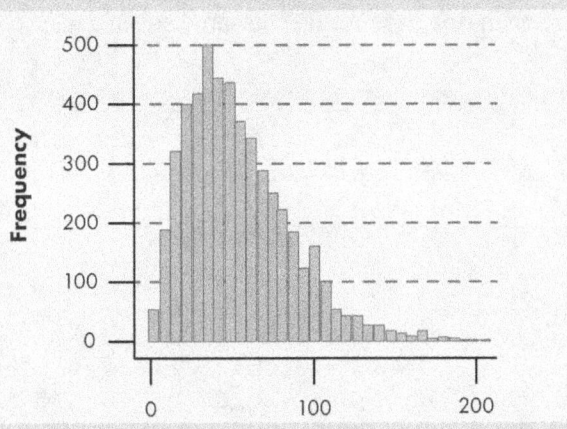

a) Skewed Left
b) Skewed Right
c) Bimodal
d) Uniform

59. Which of the following the mean of the data set?

14, 18, 11, 28, 23, 14

A) 11
B) 14
C) 18
D) 28

Data Presentation

Data can be presented in a variety of ways. In addition to a simple table, there are a number of different graphs and charts that can be used to visually represent data. The most appropriate type of graph or chart depends on the data being displayed.

Box plots (also called box and whisker plots) show data using the median, range, and outliers of a data set. They provide a helpful visual guide, showing how data is distributed around the median. In the example below, 70 is the median and the range is 0 – 100, or 100.

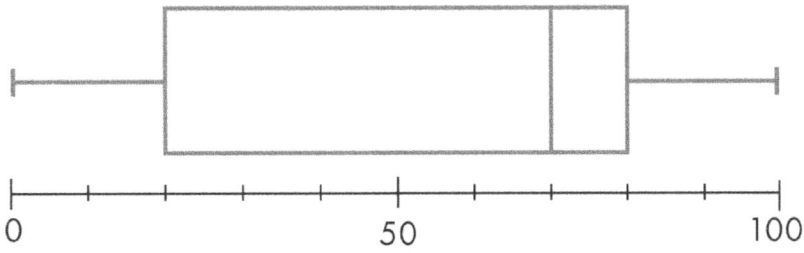

Mathematics

Bar graphs use bars of different lengths to compare data. The independent variable on a bar graph is grouped into categories such as months, flavors, or locations, and the dependent variable is a quantity. Thus, comparing the length of bars provides a visual guide to the relative amounts in each category. **Double bar graphs** show more than one data set on the same set of axes.

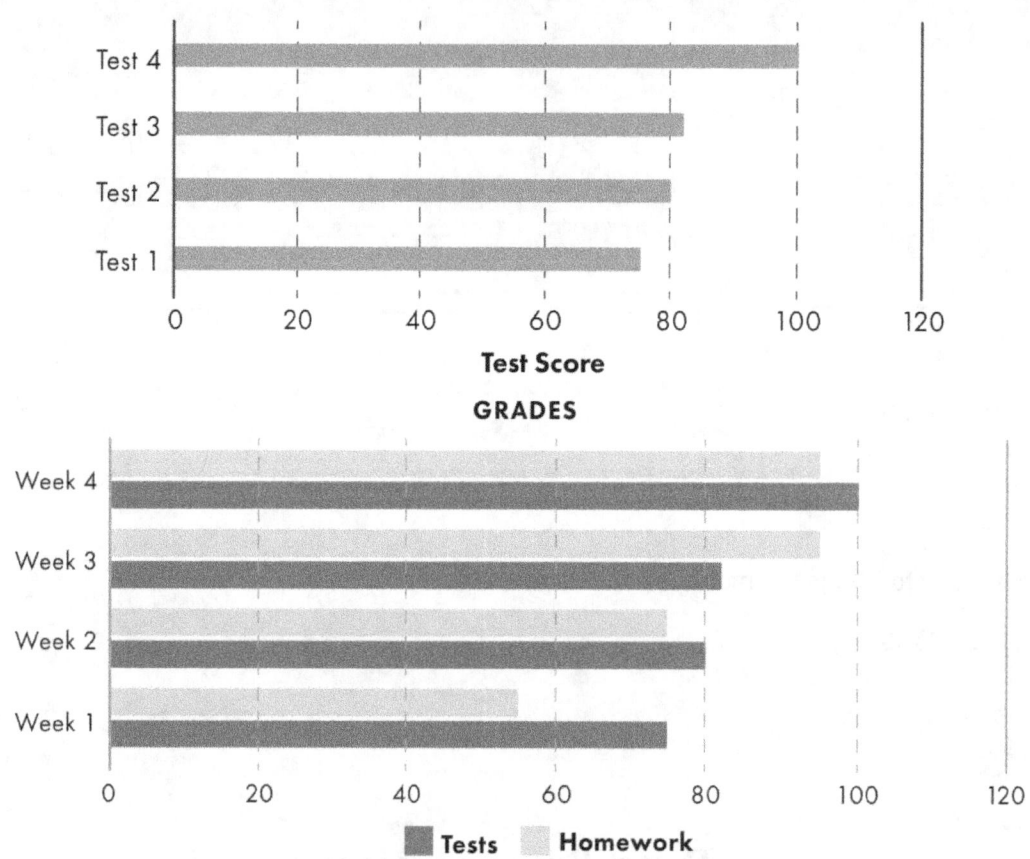

Histograms similarly use bars to compare data, but the independent variable is a continuous variable that has been "binned" or divided into categories. For example, the time of day can be broken down into 8:00 a.m. to 12:00 p.m., 12:00 p.m. to 4:00 p.m., and so on. Usually (but not always), a gap is included between the bars of a bar graph but not a histogram. The bars of a bar graph show actual data, but the bars (or bins) of a histogram show the frequency of the data in various ranges.

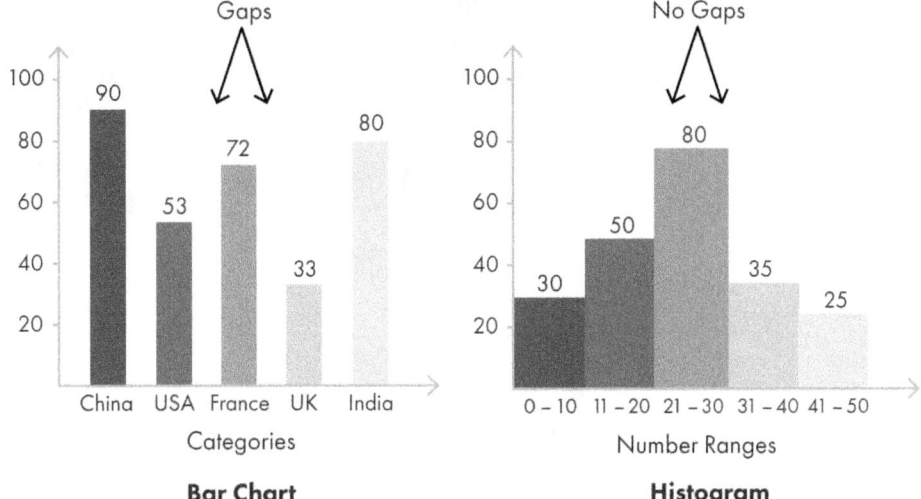

Bar Chart   **Histogram**

Dot plots display the frequency of a value or event data graphically using dots, and thus can be used to observe the distribution of a data set. Typically, a value or category is listed on the *x*-axis, and the number of times that value appears in the data set is represented by a line of vertical dots. Dot plots make it easy to see which values occur most often.

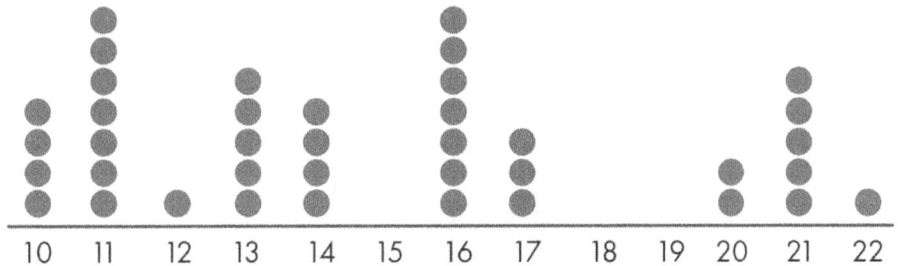

Dot plot

Scatter plots use points to show relationships between two variables which can be plotted as coordinate points. One variable describes a position on the *x*-axis, and the other a point on the *y*-axis. Scatter plots can suggest relationships between variables. For example, both variables might increase together, or one may increase when the other decreases.

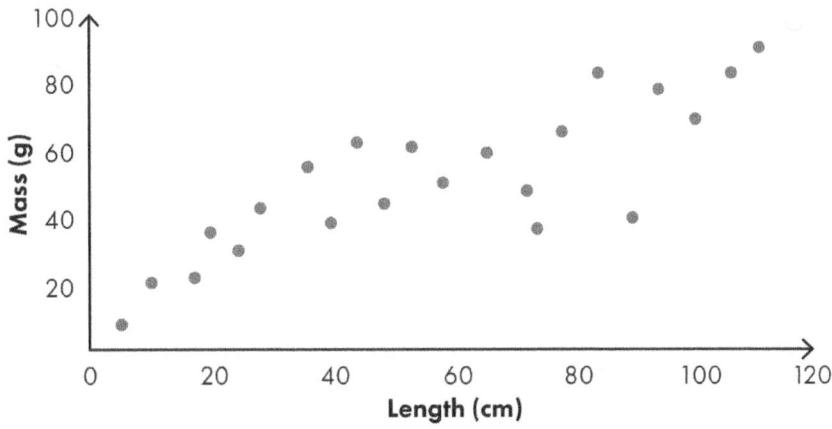

Mathematics

Line graphs show changes in data by connecting points on a scatter graph using a line. These graphs will often measure time on the *x*-axis and are used to show trends in the data, such as temperature changes over a day or school attendance throughout the year. **Double line graphs** present two sets of data on the same set of axes.

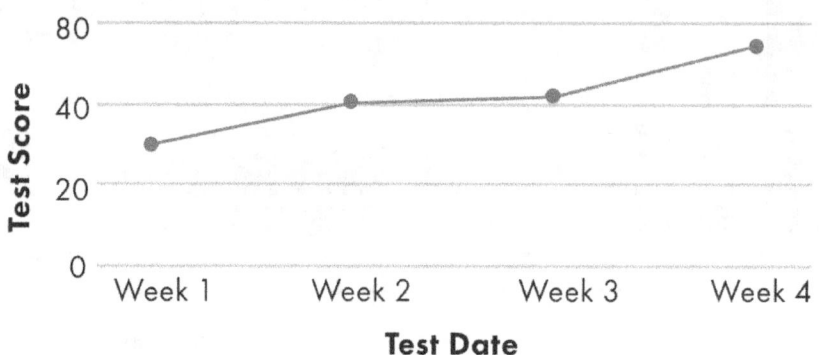

Circle graphs (also called pie charts) are used to show parts of a whole: the "pie" is the whole, and each "slice" represents a percentage or part of the whole.

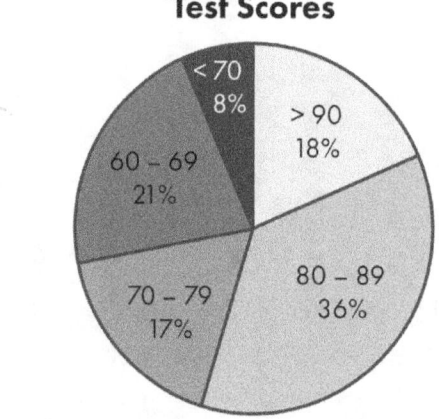

Practice Questions

60. Students are asked if they prefer vanilla, chocolate, or strawberry ice cream. The results are tallied on the following table:

Four students display the information from the table in a bar graph. Which student accurately displays the results from the survey?

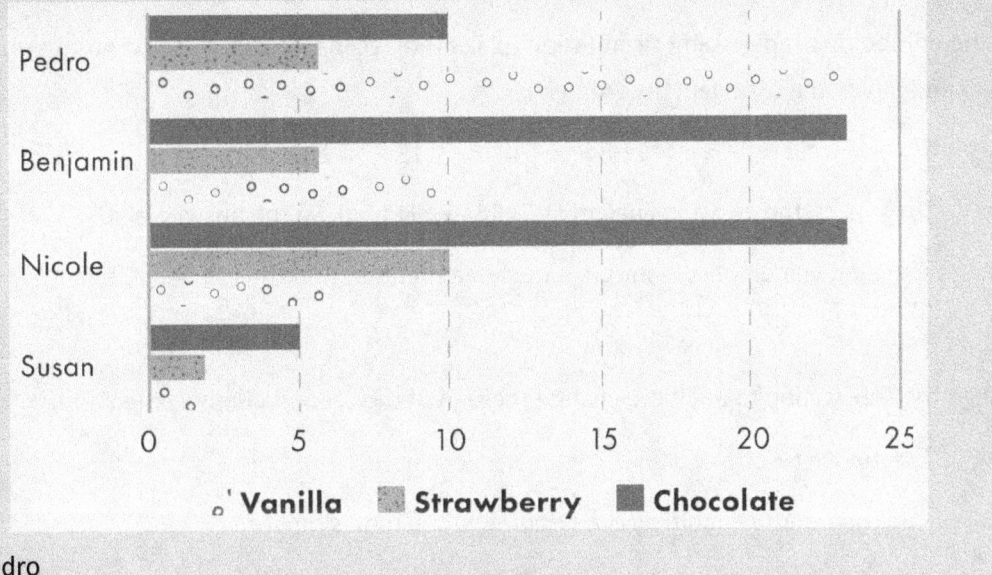

A) Pedro
B) Benjamin
C) Nicole
D) Susan

Answer Key

1. Natural, whole, integer, and rational (72 can be written as the fraction 72).

2. Rational (The number is a fraction.)

3. Irrational (The number cannot be written as a fraction, and written as a decimal it is approximately 2.2360679... Notice this decimal does not terminate, nor does it have a repeating pattern.)

4. In order to add, the exponents of 10 must be the same. Change the first number so the power of 10 is 2:

$$3.8 \times 10^3 = 3.8 \times 10 \times 10^2 = 38 \times 10^2$$

Add the terms together and write the number in proper scientific notation:

$$38 \times 10^2 + 4.7 \times 10^2 = 42.7 \times 10^2 = 4.27 \times 10^3$$

Mathematics

5. Multiply the factors and add the exponents on the base of 10:

$$(8.1 \times 1.4)(10^{-5} \times 10^7) = 11.34 \times 10^2$$

Write the number in proper scientific notation (place the decimal so that the first number is between 1 and 10 and adjust the exponent accordingly):

$$11.34 \times 10^2 = 1.134 \times 10^3$$

6. Since $|-18| > |12|$, the answer is negative. $|-18| - |12| = 6$. So the answer is −6.

7. Adding two negative numbers results in a negative number. Add the values: −5.82

8. 5.12

9. Change the subtraction to addition, change the sign of the second number, then add:

$$86 - (-20) = 86 + (+20) = 106$$

10. Multiply the numerators, multiply the denominators, then simplify:

$$-\frac{90}{15} = -6$$

11. A negative divided by a negative is a positive number:

$$-6 \cdot \frac{4}{-1} = 6.4$$

12. The parentheses indicate multiplication:

$$(-1.1)(-6.6) = 7.26$$

13. A negative divided by a positive is negative:

$$-\frac{12}{3} = -4$$

14. Calculate the expressions inside the parenthesis:

$$2(21 - 14) + 6 \div (-2) \times 3 - 10 = 2(7) + 6 \div (-2) \times 3 - 10$$

There are no exponents or radicals, so perform multiplication and division from left to right:

$$2(7) + 6 \div (-2) \times 3 - 10 = 14 + 6 \div (-2) \times 3 - 10 = 14 + (-3) \times 3 - 10$$
$$= 14 + (-9) - 10$$

Lastly, perform addition and subtraction from left to right:

$$14 + (-9) - 10 = 5 - 10 = -5$$

15. Calculate the expressions inside the parentheses:

$$-(3)^2 + 4(5) + (5 - 6)^2 - 8 = -(3)^2 + 4(5) + (-1)^2 - 8$$

Simplify exponents and radicals:

$$-(3)^2 + 4(5) + (-1)^2 - 8 = -9 + 4(5) + 1 - 8$$

Note that $-(3)^2 = -1(3)^2 = -9$ but $(-1)^2 = (-1)(-1) = 1$

Perform multiplication and division from left to right:

$$-9 + 4(5) + 1 - 8 = -9 + 20 + 1 - 8$$

Lastly, perform addition and subtraction from left to right:

$$-9 + 20 + 1 - 8 = 11 + 1 - 8 = 12 - 8 = 4$$

16. Simplify the top and bottom expressions separately using the same steps described above:

$$(-2)^3 + 8(-2) = -8 + (-16) = -24$$

$$(4^2 - 5^2) = 16 - 25 = -9$$

$$-\frac{24}{-9} = \frac{8}{3}$$

17. Apply the order of operations left to right:

$$24.38 + 16.51 = 40.89$$

$$40.89 - 29.87 = 11.02$$

18. Multiply the numbers ignoring the decimals:

$$104 \times 182 = 18,928$$

The original problem includes two decimal places (10.4 has one place after the decimal point and 18.2 has one place after the decimal point), so place the decimal point in the answer so that there are two places after the decimal point. Estimating is a good way to check the answer ($10.4 \approx 10, 18.2 \approx 18, 10 \times 18 = 180$):

$$18,928 \to 189.28$$

19. The divisor is 2.5. Move the decimal one place to the right (multiply 2.5 by 10) so that the divisor is a whole number. Since the decimal point of the divisor was moved one place to the right, the decimal point in the dividend must be moved one place to the right (multiplying it by 10 as well):

$$80 \to 800$$

$$2.5 \to 25$$

Divide normally:

$$800 \div 25 = 32$$

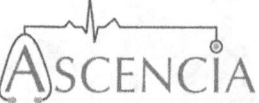

20. The first step is to change each fraction so it has a denominator of 20, which is the LCD of 5, 4, and 2:

$$2\frac{3}{5} + 3\frac{1}{4} - 1\frac{1}{2} = 2\frac{12}{20} + 3\frac{5}{20} - 1\frac{10}{20}$$

Next, add and subtract the whole numbers together and the fractions together:

$$2 + 3 - 1 = 4$$

$$\frac{12}{20} + \frac{5}{20} - \frac{10}{20} = \frac{7}{20}$$

Lastly, combine to get the final answer (a mixed number):

$$4\frac{7}{20}$$

21. Change the mixed number to an improper fraction:

$$3\frac{1}{3} = \frac{10}{3}$$

Multiply the numerators together and the denominators together, and then reduce the fraction:

$$\frac{7}{8}\left(\frac{10}{3}\right) = \frac{7 \times 10}{8 \times 3} = \frac{70}{24} = \frac{35}{12} = 2\frac{11}{12}$$

22. Change the mixed number to an improper fraction. Then, multiply the first fraction by the reciprocal of the second fraction and simplify:

$$\frac{9}{2} \div \frac{2}{3} = \frac{9}{2} \times \frac{3}{2} = \frac{27}{4} = 6\frac{3}{4}$$

23. Divide the denominator into the numerator using long division:

```
       0.875
    8 )7.0000
      -64
       ___
        60
       -56
       ___
        60
       -56
       ___
        40
       -40
       ___
         0
```

24. Dividing using long division yields a repeating decimal:

$$\begin{array}{r} 0.4545 \\ 11\overline{)5.0000} \\ -44 \\ \hline 60 \\ -55 \\ \hline 50 \\ -44 \\ \hline 60 \\ -55 \\ \hline 0 \end{array}$$

25. Place the numbers to the right of the decimal (125) in the numerator. There are three numbers, so put the number 1,000 in the denominator, and then reduce:

$$\frac{125}{1,000} = \frac{1}{8}$$

26. The 8 is in the thousands place, and the number to its right is a 4. Because 4 is less than 5, the 8 remains and all numbers to the right become zero:

$$138,472 \approx 138,000$$

27. Round each value to the thousands place and add:

$$12,341 \approx 12,000$$
$$8,975 \approx 9,000$$
$$9,431 \approx 9,000$$
$$10,521 \approx 11,000$$
$$11,427 \approx 11,000$$
$$12,000 + 9,000 + 9,000 + 11,000 + 11,000 = 52,000$$

28. There are 22 total students in the class. The ratio can be written as $\frac{10}{22}$, and reduced to $\frac{5}{11}$. The ratio of girls to boys is 12:10 or 6:5.

29. The family's total expenses for the month add up to $2,300. The ratio of the rent to total amount of expenses can be written as $\frac{600}{2,300}$ and reduced to $\frac{6}{23}$.

30. Start by cross multiplying:

$$\frac{3-5}{2} = \frac{-8}{3} \rightarrow 3(3-5x) = 2(-8)$$

Mathematics

Then, solve the equation:

$$9 - 15x = -16$$

$$-15x = -25$$

$$x = \frac{-25}{-15} = \frac{5}{3}$$

31. Write a proportion where x equals the actual distance and each ratio is written as inches:miles:

$$\frac{2.5}{40} = \frac{17.25}{x}$$

Then, cross-multiply and divide to solve:

$$2.5x = 690$$

$$x = 276$$

The two cities are 276 miles apart.

32. Write a proportion in which x is the number of defective parts made and both ratios are written as defective parts:total parts:

$$\frac{4}{1,000} = \frac{x}{125,000}$$

Then, cross-multiply and divide to solve for x:

$$1,000x = 500,000$$

$$x = 500$$

There are 500 defective parts for the month.

33. The percent is written as a fraction over 100 and reduced:

$$\frac{18}{100} = \frac{9}{50}$$

34. Dividing 5 by 3 gives the value 0.6, which is then multiplied by 100: 60%

35. The decimal point is moved two places to the right:

$$1.125 = 112.5\%$$

36. The decimal point is moved two places to the left:

$$84\% = 0.84$$

37. The first step is to find the percent of students who are girls by subtracting from 100%:

$$100\% - 54\% = 46\%$$

Next, identify the variables and plug into the appropriate equation:

$$percent = 46\% = 0.46$$

$$whole = 650 \; students$$

$$part = ?$$

$$part = whole \times percent = 0.46 \times 650 = 299$$

There are 299 girls.

38. The first step is to identify the necessary values. These can then be plugged into the appropriate equation:

$$original \; amount = 1{,}500$$

$$percent \; change = 45\% = 0.45$$

$$of \; change = ?$$

$$amount \; of \; change = original \; amount \times percent \; change = 1{,}500 \times 0.45 = 675$$

To find the new price, subtract the amount of change from the original price:

$$1{,}500 - 675 = 825$$

The final price is $825.

39. Identify the necessary values and plug into the appropriate equation:

$$original \; amount = 100{,}000$$

$$amount \; of \; change = 120{,}000 - 100{,}000 = 20{,}000$$

$$percent \; change = ?$$

$$\frac{amount \; of \; change}{original \; amount} = \frac{20{,}000}{100{,}000}$$

To find the percent growth, multiply by 100:

$$0.20 \times 100 = 20\%$$

40. Change each fraction to a decimal:

$$-\frac{2}{3} = -0.\overline{66}$$

$$\frac{4}{3} = 1.25$$

$$\frac{1}{8} = 0.125$$

Mathematics

Now place the decimals in order from greatest to least:

$$1.25, 1.2, 0.125, 0, -0.\overline{66}, -1, -2.1$$

Lastly, convert back to fractions if the problem requires it:

$$\frac{5}{4}, 1.2, \frac{1}{8}, 0, -\frac{2}{3}, -1, -2.1$$

41. Convert each value using the least common denominator value of 24:

$$\frac{1}{3} = \frac{8}{24}$$

$$-\frac{5}{6} = -\frac{20}{24}$$

$$1\frac{1}{8} = \frac{9}{8} = \frac{27}{24}$$

$$\frac{7}{12} = \frac{14}{24}$$

$$-\frac{3}{4} = -\frac{18}{24}$$

$$-\frac{3}{2} = -\frac{36}{24}$$

Next, put the fractions in order from least to greatest by comparing the numerators:

$$-\frac{36}{24}, -\frac{20}{24}, -\frac{18}{24}, \frac{8}{24}, \frac{14}{24}, \frac{27}{24}$$

Finally, put the fractions back in their original form if the problem requires it:

$$-\frac{3}{2}, -\frac{5}{6}, -\frac{3}{4}, \frac{1}{3}, \frac{7}{12}, 1\frac{1}{8}$$

42. First, plug the value 4 in for m in the expression:

$$5(m-2)^3 + 3m^2 - \frac{m}{4} - 1$$

$$= 5(4-2)^3 + 3(4)^2 - \frac{4}{4} - 1$$

Then, simplify using PEMDAS:

$$P: 5(2)^3 + 3(4)^2 - \frac{4}{4} - 1$$

$$E: = 5(8) + 3(16) - \frac{3}{3}$$

M and D, working left to right: $= 40 + 48 - 1$

A and S, working left to right: 86

1. The only like terms in both expressions are 12x and 8x, so these two terms will be added, and all other terms will remain the same:

$$a + b = (12x + 8x) + 7xy - 9y - 9xz + 7z$$
$$= 20x + 7xy - 9y - 9xz + 7z$$

2. The term outside the parentheses must be distributed and multiplied by all three terms inside the parentheses:

$$(5x)(x^2) = 5x^3$$
$$(5x)(-2c) = -10xc$$
$$(5x)(10) = 50x$$
$$5x(x^2 - 2c + 10) \to 5x^3 - 10xc + 50x$$

3. Start by distributing for each set of parentheses:

$$x(5 + z) - z(4x - z^2)$$

Notice that $-z$ is distributed and that $(-z)(-z^2) = +z^3$. Failing to distribute the negative is a very common error.

$$5x + xz - 4zx + z^3$$

Note that xz is a like term with zx (commutative property), and they can therefore be combined.

Now combine like terms and place terms in the appropriate order (highest exponents first):

$$z^3 - 3xz + 5x$$

4. To cancel out the denominator, multiply both sides by 20:

$$20 \frac{100(x + 5)}{20} = 1 \times 20$$
$$100(x + 5) = 20$$

Next, distribute 100 through the parentheses:

$$100(x + 5) = 20$$
$$100x + 500 = 20$$

"Undo" the +500 by subtracting 500 from both sides of the equation to isolate the variable term:

$$100x = -480$$

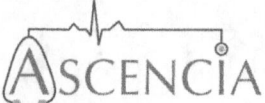

Finally, "undo" the multiplication by 100: divide by 100 on both sides to solve for x:

$$x = -\frac{480}{100} = -4.8$$

5. First, simplify the left-hand side of the equation using order of operations and combining like terms.

$$2(x + 2)^2 - 2x^2 + 10 = 20$$

Do the exponent first:

$$2(x + 2)(x + 2) - 2x^2 + 10 = 20$$

FOIL:

$$2(x^2 + 4x + 4) - 2x^2 + 10 = 20$$

Distribute the 2:

$$2x^2 + 8x + 8 - 2x^2 + 10 = 20$$

Combine like terms on the left-hand side:

$$8x + 18 = 20$$

Now, isolate the variable.

"Undo" +18 by subtracting 18 from both sides:

$$8x + 18 = 20$$
$$8x = 2$$

"Undo" multiplication by 8 by dividing both sides by 8:

$$x = \frac{2}{8} = \frac{1}{4}$$

6. The y-intercept can be identified on the graph as (0, 3). Thus, $b = 3$.

To find the slope, choose any two points and plug the values into the slope equation. The two points chosen here are (2, −1) and (3, −3).

$$m = \frac{(-3) - (-1)}{3 - 2} = -\frac{2}{1} = -2$$

Replace m with −2 and b with 3 in $y = mx + b$. The equation of the line is $y = -2x + 3$.

7. Rearrange the equation into slope-intercept form by solving the equation for y. Isolate −2y by subtracting 6x and adding 8 to both sides of the equation.

$$-2y = -6x + 8$$

Divide both sides by −2:

$$y = (-6x + 8) / -2$$

Simplify the fraction:

$$y = 3x - 4$$

The slope is 3, since it is the coefficient of x.

8. The problem is asking for the number of tickets. First, identify the quantities:

$$\text{number of tickets} = x$$
$$\text{cost per ticket} = 5$$
$$\text{cost for x tickets} = 5x$$
$$\text{total cost} = 28$$
$$\text{entry fee} = 3$$

Now, set up an equation. The total cost for x tickets will be equal to the cost for x tickets plus the $3 entry fee:

$$5x + 3 = 28$$

Now solve the equation:

$$5x + 3 = 28$$
$$5x = 25$$
$$x = 5$$

The student bought 5 tickets.

9. The problem asks for the number of hours Abby will have to work. First, identify the quantities:

$$\text{number of hours} = x$$
$$\text{amount earned per hour} = 10$$
$$\text{amount of money earned} = 10x$$
$$\text{price of bicycle} = 395$$
$$\text{money borrowed} = 150$$

Now, set up an equation. The amount of money she has borrowed plus the money she earned as a waitress needs to equal the cost of the bicycle:

$$10x + 150 = 395$$

Mathematics

Now solve the equation:

$$10x + 150 = 395$$
$$10x = 245$$
$$x = 24.5 \text{ hours}$$

She will need to work 24.5 hours.

10. Inequalities can be solved using the same steps used to solve equations. Start by subtracting 10 from both sides:

$$4x + 10 > 58$$
$$4x > 48$$

Now divide by 4 to isolate x:

$$x > 12$$

11. They have to spend less than $2,500 on uniforms, so this problem is an inequality. First, identify the quantities:

$$\text{number of t} - \text{shirts} = t$$
$$\text{total cost of t} - \text{shirts} = 12t$$
$$\text{number of pants} = p$$
$$\text{total cost of pants} = 15p$$
$$\text{number of pairs of shoes} = s$$
$$\text{total cost of shoes} = 45s$$

The cost of all the items must be less than $2,500:

$$12t + 15p + 45s < 2,500$$

12. $4.25 \, km \left(\dfrac{1,000 \, m}{1 \, km}\right) = 4,250 \, m$

13. $12 \, ft \left(\dfrac{12 \, in}{1 \, ft}\right) = 144 \, in$

14. The figure can be broken apart into three rectangles:

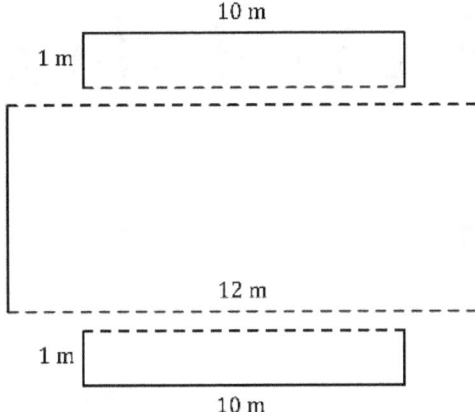

The area of each smaller rectangle is $1\,m \times 10\,m = 10\,m^2$. The area of the larger rectangle is $10\,m \times 12\,m = 120\,m^2$. Together, the area of the three shapes is $10\,m^2 + 120\,m^2 = 140\,m^2$.

$$10\,m^2 + 10\,m^2 + 120\,m^2 = 140\,m^2$$

15. The area of the shaded region is the area of the rectangle minus the area of the triangle:

$$\text{rectangle} - \text{triangle} = (8\,ft \times 16\,ft) - (0.5 \times 8\,ft \times 6\,ft) = 128\,ft^2 - 24\,ft^2 = 104\,ft^2$$

16. **B:** The graph is skewed right because there are fewer data points on the right half.

17. **C:** The mean is the average:

$$\frac{(14 + 18 + 11 + 28 + 23 + 14)}{6} = \frac{108}{6} = 18$$

18. **B:** Benjamin's bar graph indicates that ten students prefer vanilla, six students prefer strawberry, and twenty-three students prefer chocolate ice cream.

Anatomy and Physiology

Anatomical Terminology

The Biological Hierarchy

Organisms are living things consisting of at least one cell, which is the smallest unit of life that can reproduce on its own. Unicellular organisms, such as the amoeba, are made up of only one cell, while multicellular organisms are comprised of many cells. In a multicellular organism, the cells are grouped together into **tissues**, and these tissues are grouped into **organs**, which perform a specific function. The heart, for example, is the organ that pumps blood throughout the body. Organs are further grouped into **organ systems**, such as the digestive or respiratory systems.

A system is a collection of interconnected parts that make up a complex whole with defined boundaries. Systems may be closed, meaning nothing passes in or out of them, or open, meaning they have inputs and outputs. Organ systems are open and will have a number of inputs and outputs.

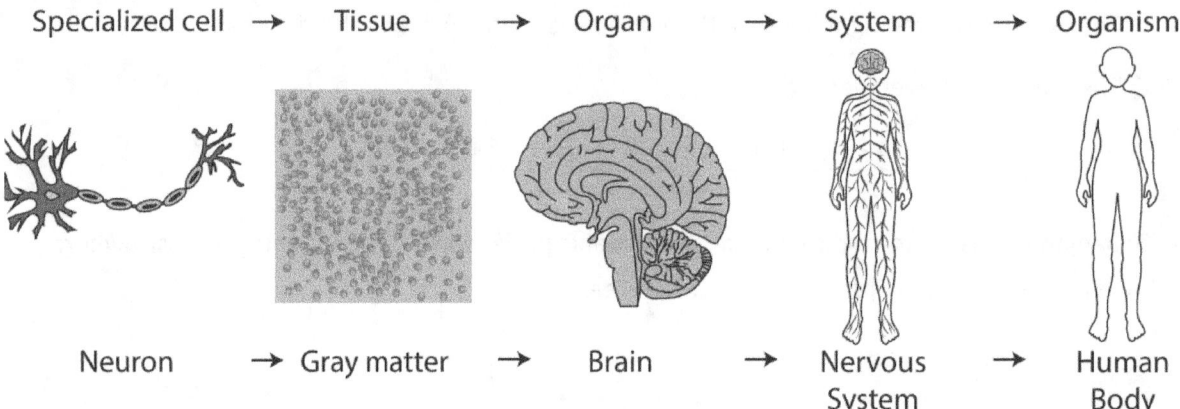

Specialized cell → Tissue → Organ → System → Organism

Neuron → Gray matter → Brain → Nervous System → Human Body

Directional Terms

Learning anatomy requires an understanding of the terminology used to describe the location of a particular structure. Anatomical science uses common terms to describe spatial relationships, often in pairs of opposites. These terms usually refer to the position of a structure in an organism that is upright with respect to its environment (e.g., in its typical orientation while moving forward).

Table 3.1. Directional Terms		
Term	Meaning	Example
Inferior	away from the head	The pelvis is inferior to the head.

Table 3.1. Directional Terms

Term	Meaning	Example
Superior	closer to the head	The head is superior to the pelvis.
Anterior	toward the front	The eyes are anterior to the ears.
Posterior	toward the back	The ears are posterior to the eyes.
Ventral	toward the front	The stomach is ventral to the spine.
Dorsal	toward the back	The spine is dorsal to the stomach.
Medial	toward the midline of the body	The heart is medial to the arm.
Lateral	further from the midline of the body	The arm is lateral to the chest.
Proximal	closer to the trunk	The knee is proximal to the ankle.
Distal	away from the trunk	The ankle is distal to the knee.

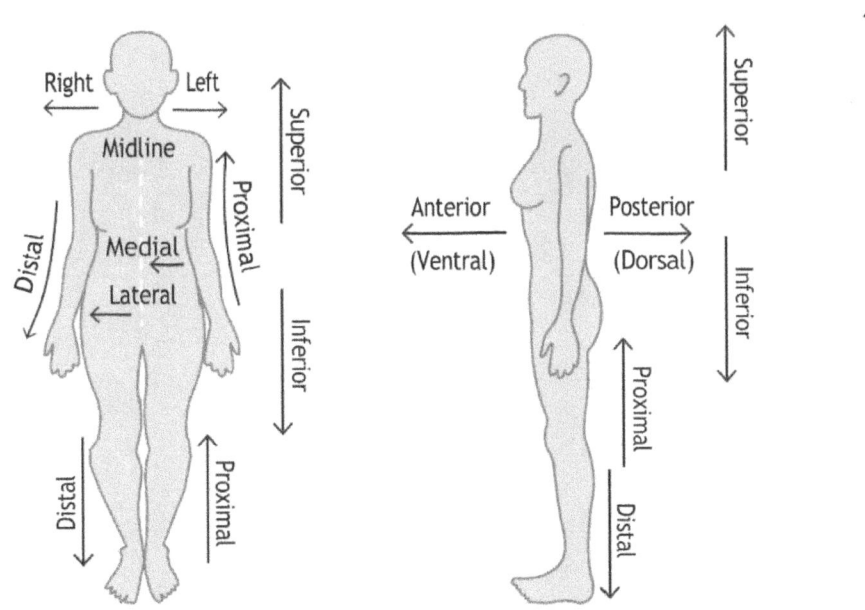

Body Cavities

The internal structure of the human body is organized into compartments called **cavities**, which are separated by membranes. There are two main cavities in the human body: the dorsal cavity and the ventral cavity (both named for their relative positions).

The **dorsal cavity** is further divided into the **cranial cavity**, which holds the brain, and the **spinal cavity**, which surrounds the spine. The two sections of the dorsal cavity are continuous with each other. Both sections are lined by the **meninges**, a three-layered membrane that protects the brain and spinal cord.

The **ventral cavity** houses the majority of the body's organs. It also can be further divided into smaller cavities. The **thoracic cavity** holds the heart and lungs, the **abdominal cavity** holds the digestive organs and kidneys, and the **pelvic cavity** holds the bladder and reproductive organs. Both the abdominal and pelvic cavities are enclosed by a membrane called the **peritoneum**.

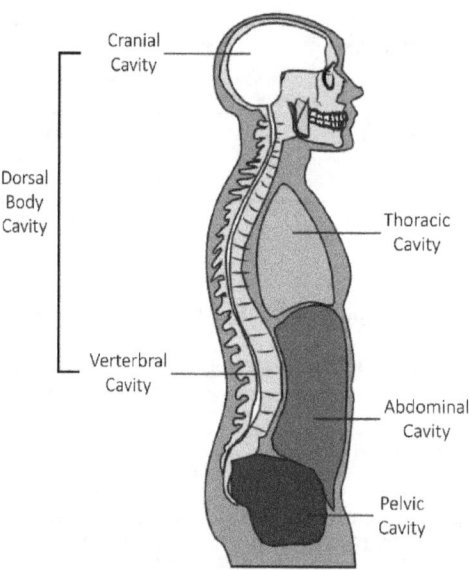

Practice Questions

1. Which term means *above*?
    A) anterior
    B) posterior
    C) superior
    D) medial

2. Where is the wrist located relative to the elbow?
    A) distal
    B) proximal
    C) anterior
    D) posterior

The Respiratory System

Structure and Function of the Respiratory System

Mammalian cells require oxygen for glucose metabolism and release carbon dioxide as a byproduct. This process requires constant gas exchange between the human body and the environment to replenish the oxygen supply and remove carbon dioxide. This exchange is accomplished through the efforts of the **respiratory system**, in which powerful muscles force oxygen-rich air into the lungs and carbon dioxide-rich air out of the body.

> **HELPFUL HINT**
>
> In anatomy, the terms *right* and *left* are used with respect to the subject, not the observer.

Gas exchange takes place in the **lungs**. Humans have two lungs, a right and a left, with the right being slightly larger than the left due to the heart's placement in the left side of the chest cavity. The right lung has three **lobes**, and the left has two. The lungs are surrounded by a thick membrane called the **pleura**.

Air enters the body through the mouth or nasal cavity and passes through the **trachea** (sometimes called the windpipe) and into the two bronchi, each of which leads to one lung. Within the lung, the bronchi branch into smaller passageways called **bronchioles** and then terminate in sac-like structures called **alveoli**, which is where gas exchange between the air and the capillaries occurs. The large surface area of the alveoli allows for efficient exchange of gases through diffusion (movement of particles from areas of high to low concentration). Alveoli are covered in a layer of **surfactant**, which lubricates the sacs and prevents the lungs from collapsing.

The heart pumps deoxygenated blood into the lungs via the **pulmonary artery**. This blood is oxygenated in the alveoli and then delivered back into the heart by the **pulmonary veins** for distribution to the body.

> **QUICK REVIEW**
>
> How might measuring tidal volume and residual capacity help evaluate respiratory health?

The **diaphragm** contributes to the activity of ventilation—the process of inhalation and exhalation. The contraction of the diaphragm creates a vacuum, forcing air into the lungs. Relaxation of the diaphragm compresses the lungs, forcing carbon dioxide-enriched gas out in exhalation. The amount of air breathed in and out is the **tidal volume**, and the **residual capacity** is the small volume of air left in the lungs after exhalation.

Pathologies of the Respiratory System

The body's critical and constant need for the exchange of carbon dioxide for oxygen makes the pulmonary system a locus of many serious diseases. Lung diseases that result in the continual restriction of airflow are known as **chronic obstructive pulmonary disease (COPD)**. These include **emphysema**, which is the destruction of lung tissues, and **asthma**, in which the airways are compromised due to a dysfunctional immune response. The main causes of COPD are smoking and air pollution, but genetic factors can also influence the severity of the disease.

The system is also prone to **respiratory tract infections**, with upper respiratory tract infections affecting air inputs in the nose and throat and lower respiratory tract infections affecting the lungs and their immediate pulmonary inputs. Viral infections of the respiratory system include influenza and the common cold; bacterial infections include tuberculosis and pertussis (whooping cough). **Pneumonia**, which affects alveoli, is a bacterial or viral infection that is often seen in people whose respiratory system has been weakened by other conditions.

Practice Questions

3. Which of the following structures are small air sacs that function as the site of gas exchange in the lungs?
    A) capillaries
    B) bronchi
    C) alveoli
    D) cilia

4. Which of the following conditions is caused by an immune response?
    A) COPD
    B) influenza
    C) asthma
    D) emphysema

The Cardiovascular System

Structure and Function of the Cardiovascular System

The cardiovascular system circulates blood throughout the body. Blood carries a wide range of molecules necessary for the body to function, including nutrients, wastes, hormones, and gases. Blood is broken into a number of different parts. Red blood cells, which contain the protein **hemoglobin**, transport oxygen, and white blood cells circulate as part of the immune system. Both red and white blood cells are suspended in a fluid called **plasma**, which the other molecules transported by the blood are dissolved in.

Blood is circulated by a muscular organ called the **heart**. The circulatory system includes two closed loops. In the pulmonary loop, deoxygenated blood leaves the heart and travels to the lungs, where it loses carbon dioxide and becomes rich in oxygen. The oxygenated blood then returns to the heart, which pumps it through the systemic loop. The systemic loop delivers oxygen to the rest of the body and returns deoxygenated blood to the heart. The pumping action of the heart is regulated primarily by two neurological nodes, the **sinoatrial** and **atrioventricular nodes**, whose electrical activity sets the rhythm of the heart.

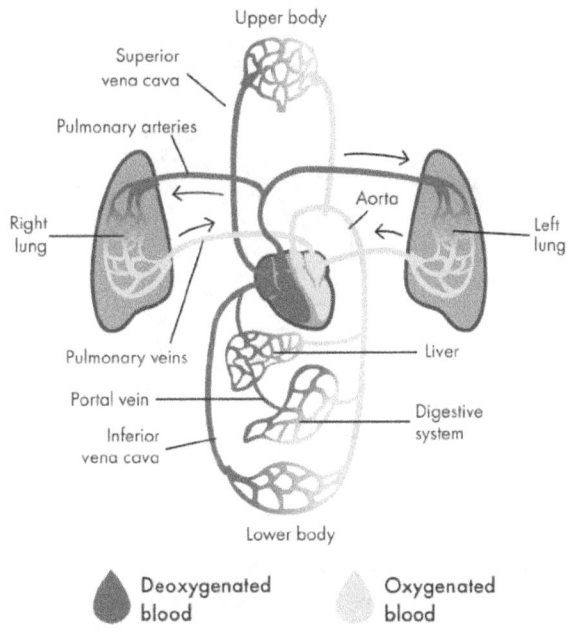

Deoxygenated blood from the body enters the heart via the **right atrium**. It then passes through the **tricuspid** valve into the **right ventricle** and is pumped out to the lungs. Oxygenated blood returns from the lungs into the **left atrium**. It then passes through the **mitral valve** into the **left ventricle** and is pumped out to the body through the **aorta**. The contraction of the heart during this process is called **systole**, and the relaxation of the heart is **diastole**.

Blood is carried through the body in a system of blood vessels. Oxygenated blood leaves the heart in large vessels called **arteries**, which branch into smaller and smaller vessels. The smallest vessels, **capillaries**, are where the exchange of molecules between blood and cells takes place. Deoxygenated blood returns to the heart in **veins**.

HELPFUL HINT

The pulmonary veins are the only veins in the human body that carry oxygenated blood.

Blood leaves the heart to travel to the body through the **aorta**; in the lower body, the aorta branches into the **iliac arteries**. Deoxygenated blood returns to the heart from the body via the **superior vena cava** (upper body) and **inferior vena cava** (lower body). Blood then leaves the heart again to travel to the lungs through the **pulmonary arteries**, and returns from the lungs via the **pulmonary veins**.

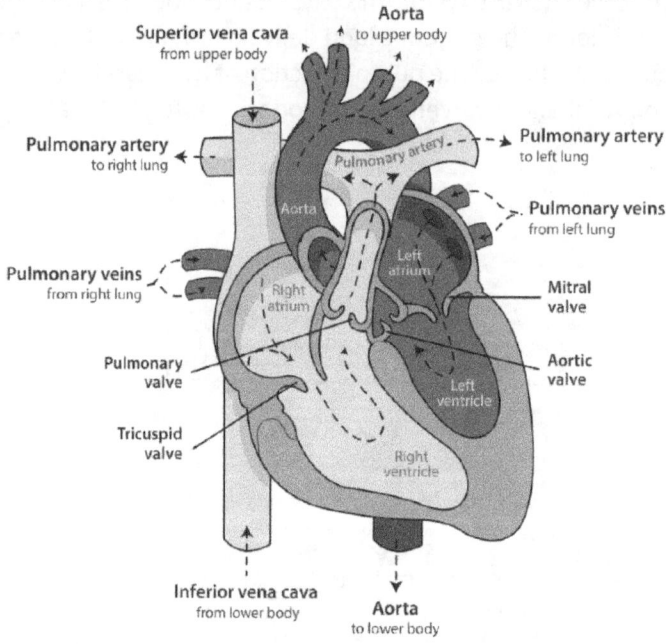

The Lymphatic System

The **lymphatic system** is an open circulatory system that functions alongside the cardiovascular system. It facilitates the movement of substances between cells and the blood by removing interstitial fluid (the fluid between cells). It also plays an important role in the immune system by circulating white blood cells. The system is composed of **lymphatic vessels** that carry **lymph**, a clear fluid containing lymphocytes and waste products. Lymph passes through **lymph nodes**, which are collections of tissue rich in white blood cells that filter out harmful substances such as pathogens and cell waste. The lymph is then returned to the circulatory system through the veins near the heart.

> **HELPFUL HINT**
>
> Lymph nodes can become inflamed during infections when they contain a higher-than-normal number of lymphocytes.

Pathologies of the Cardiovascular System

The cardiovascular system is subject to a number of pathologies. In a **heart attack**, blood flow to part of the heart is stopped, causing damage to the heart muscle. An irregular heartbeat, called an **arrhythmia**, is caused by disruptions with the electrical signals in the heart. Many arrhythmias can be treated—with a pacemaker, for example—or do not cause any symptoms.

Problems with blood vessels include **atherosclerosis**, in which white blood cells and plaque build up in arteries, and **hypertension**, or high blood pressure. In a stroke, blood flow is blocked in the brain, resulting in damage to brain cells.

Practice Questions

5. The mitral valve transports blood between which of the following two regions of the heart?
   A) aorta and left atrium
   B) aorta and right atrium
   C) right atrium and right ventricle
   D) left atrium and left ventricle

6. Which of the following supplies blood to the lower body?
   A) superior vena cava
   B) inferior vena cava
   C) iliac artery
   D) aortic arch

7. Which of the following electrically signals the heart to pump?
   A) sinoatrial node
   B) aorta
   C) mitral valve
   D) left ventricle

The Nervous System

The nervous system is made up of two distinct parts: the central nervous system (brain and spinal cord) and the peripheral nervous system. However, the fundamental physiological principles underlying both systems are similar. In both systems, **neurons** communicate electrically and chemically with one another along pathways. These pathways allow the nervous system as a whole to conduct its incredibly broad array of functions, from motor control and sensory perception to complex thinking and emotions.

> **HELPFUL HINT**
>
> Nerve cell signaling is controlled by moving ions across the cell membrane to maintain an action potential. Depolarizing the cell, or lowering the action potential, triggers the release of neurotransmitters.

Never Cells

Neurons, a.k.a. nerve cells, have several key anatomical features that contribute to their specialized functions. These cells typically contain an **axon**, a long projection from the cell that sends information over a distance. These cells also have **dendrites**, which are long, branching extensions of the cell that receive information from neighboring cells. The number of dendrites and the extent of their branching varies widely, distinguishing the various types of these cells.

Neurons and nerve cells do not touch; instead, communication occurs across a specialized gap called a **synapse**. The chemicals that facilitate communication across synapses are known as **neurotransmitters**, and include serotonin and dopamine. Communication occurs when electrical signals cause the **axon terminal** to release neurotransmitters.

Nerve cells are accompanied by glia, or supporting cells, that surround the cell and provide support, protection, and nutrients. In the peripheral nervous system, the primary glial cell is a **Schwann cell**. Schwann cells secrete a fatty substance called **myelin** that wraps around the neuron and allows much faster transmission of the electrical signal the neuron is sending. Gaps in the myelin sheath are called nodes of Ranvier.

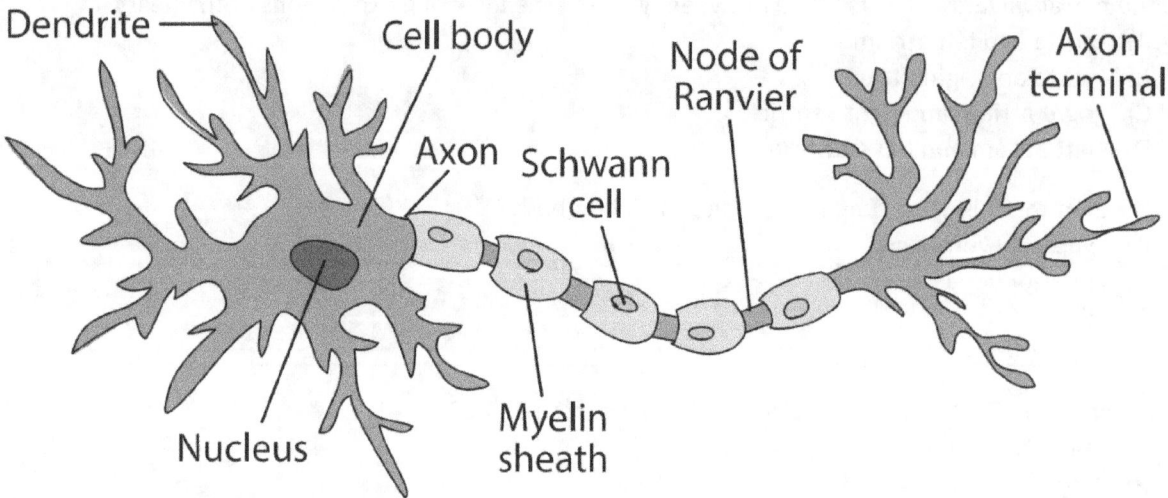

The Central Nervous System

The central nervous system (CNS), which includes the brain and spinal cord, is responsible for arguably the body's most complex and abstract functions, including cognition, emotion, and behavioral regulation. The brain is divided into six general regions:

- cerebrum: the largest part of the brain; responsible for voluntary movement, language, learning, and memory
- diencephalon: includes the thalamus, hypothalamus, and pineal body; relays sensory information and controls some automatic functions of the peripheral nervous system
- mesencephalon (midbrain): processes hearing and visual information; maintains sleep/wake cycles and temperature
- pons: controls many involuntary processes, including respiration, bladder control, and sleep; also responsible for facial movements and eye movement
- cerebellum: responsible for motor control and motor learning
- medulla oblongata: controls involuntary processes of the cardiac and respiratory systems; responsible for reflexes such as sneezing and vomiting

> **HELPFUL HINT**
>
> The "fight or flight" reaction includes accelerated breathing and heart rate, dilation of blood vessels in muscles, release of energy molecules for use by muscles, relaxation of the bladder, and slowing or stopping movement in the upper digestive tract.

The cerebrum and cerebellum are further broken down into **lobes** that each carry out a broad common function. For example, in the cerebrum, the processing of visual information occurs in the **occipital lobe,** and the **temporal lobe** is involved in language comprehension and emotional associations.

In addition to its organization by lobes and structures, regions of the brain are also designated by myelination status: **white matter** regions are myelinated and **gray matter** regions are unmyelinated.

Brain structures in the cerebral cortex (the outermost brain layer) form a convoluted pattern of **gyri** (ridges) and **sulci** (valleys) that maximize the ratio of surface area to volume.

The Peripheral Nervous System

The peripheral nervous system, which includes all the nerve cells outside the brain and spinal cord, has one main function and that is to communicate between the CNS and the rest of the body.

> **HELPFUL HINT**
>
> Alzheimer's disease, which causes dementia, is the result of damaged neurons in the cerebral cortex, the area of the brain responsible for higher order functions like information processing and language.

The peripheral nervous system is further divided into two systems. The **automatic nervous system** (ANS) is the part of the peripheral nervous system that controls involuntary bodily functions such as digestion, respiration, and heart rate. The autonomic nervous system is further broken down into the sympathetic nervous system and parasympathetic nervous system.

The **sympathetic nervous system** is responsible for the body's reaction to stress and induces a "fight or flight" response to stimuli. For instance, if an individual is frightened, the sympathetic nervous system increases the person's heart rate and blood pressure to prepare that person to either fight or flee.

In contrast, the **parasympathetic nervous system** is stimulated by the body's need for rest or recovery. The parasympathetic nervous system responds by decreasing heart rate, blood pressure, and muscular activation when a person is getting ready for activities such as sleeping or digesting food. For example, the body activates the parasympathetic nervous system after a person eats a large meal, which is why that individual may then feel sluggish.

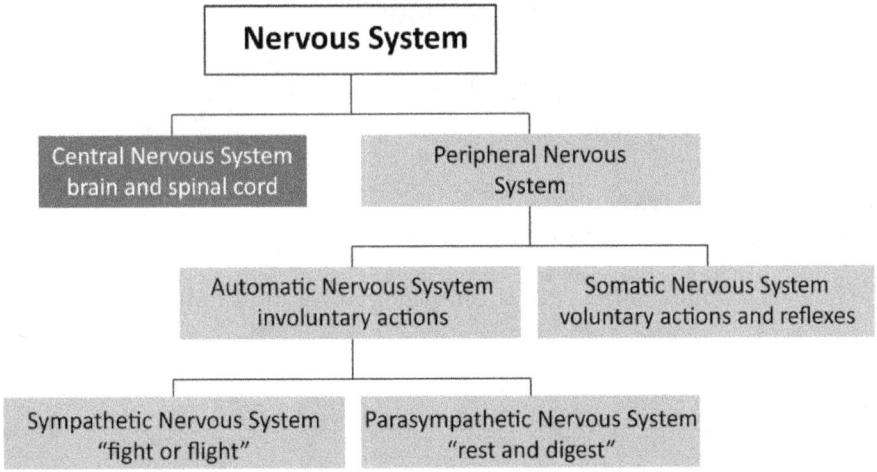

The second part of the peripheral nervous system, called the **somatic nervous system**, controls sensory information and motor control. Generally, nerve cells can be divided into two types. **Afferent** (sensory) cells relay messages to the central nervous system, and **efferent** (motor) cells carry messages to the muscles. In the motor nervous system, signals from the brain travel down the spinal cord before exiting and communicating with motor nerve cells, which synapse on muscle fibers at **neuromuscular junctions**. Because individuals can control the movement of skeletal muscle, this part of the nervous system is considered voluntary.

Some **reflexes**, or automatic response to stimuli, are able to occur rapidly by bypassing the brain altogether. In a **reflex arc**, a signal is sent from the peripheral nervous system to the spinal cord, which then sends a signal directly to a motor cells, causing movement.

Pathologies of the Nervous System

The nervous system can be affected by a number of degenerative diseases that result from the gradual breakdown of nervous tissue. These include:

- Parkinson's disease: caused by cell death in the basal ganglia; characterized by gradual loss of motor function
- multiple sclerosis (MS): caused by damage to the myelin sheath; characterized by muscle spasms and weakness, numbness, loss of coordination, and blindness
- amyotrophic lateral sclerosis (ALS): caused by the death of neurons that control voluntary muscle movement; characterized by muscle stiffness, twitches, and weakness
- Alzheimer's disease: caused by damaged neurons in the cerebral cortex; characterized by memory loss, confusion, mood swings, and problems with language

The nervous system is also susceptible to infections, some of which can be life threatening. **Meningitis** is inflammation of the meninges, the protective membrane that surrounds the brain and spinal cord, and **encephalitis** is inflammation of the brain. Both conditions can be caused by viral or bacterial pathogens.

Epileptic seizures are brief episodes caused by disturbed or overactive nerve cell activity in the brain. Seizures range widely in severity and may include confusion, convulsions, and loss of consciousness. They have many causes, including tumors, infections, head injuries, and medications.

Practice Questions

8. Which prat of the nervous system controls only voluntary action?
    A) the peripheral nervous system
    B) the somatic nervous system
    C) the sympathetic nervous system
    D) the parasympathetic nervous system

9. Which of the following is the part of a nerve cell that receives information?
    A) axon
    B) dendrite
    C) Schwann cell
    D) myelin

The Gastrointestinal System

Structure and Function of the Gastrointestinal System

Fueling the biological systems mentioned previously is the digestive system. The digestive system is essentially a continuous tube in which food is processed. During digestion, the body extracts necessary nutrients and biological fuels and isolates waste to be discarded.

The breakdown of food into its constituent parts begins as soon as it is put into the mouth. Enzymes in **saliva** such as salivary amylase begin breaking down food, particularly starch, as mastication helps prepare food for swallowing and subsequent digestion. Food from this point is formed into a **bolus** that travels down the esophagus, aided by a process called **peristalsis**, rhythmic contractions that move the partially digested food towards the stomach. Upon reaching the **stomach**, food encounters a powerful acid (composed mainly of hydrochloric acid), which aids the breakdown of food into its absorbable components.

> **HELPFUL HINT**
> The burning sensation called heartburn occurs when gastric acid from the stomach travels up the esophagus, often as a result of relaxation of the lower esophageal sphincter. This acid can damage the lining of the esophagus.

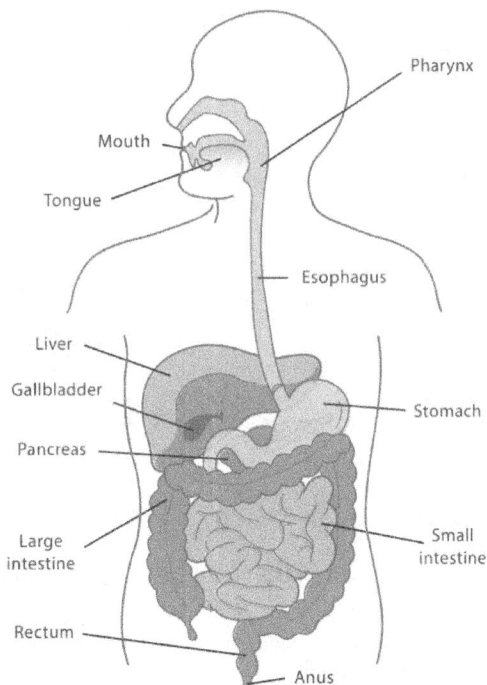

The human body derives fuel primarily from three sources: proteins, sugars, and fats (lipids). Enzymes break proteins down into their constituent amino acids to produce new proteins for the body. Carbohydrates are broken down enzymatically if necessary and used for metabolism. Fats are broken down into constituent fatty acids and glycerol for a number of uses, including dense nutritional energy storage. Digestion of fat requires **bile** acids produced by the **liver**; bile is stored in the **gall bladder**.

The stomach produces a semifluid mass of partially digested food called **chyme** that passes into the **small intestine**, where nutrients are absorbed into the bloodstream. This absorption occurs through millions of finger-like projections known as **villi** that increase the surface area available for the absorption of nutrients.

The small intestine itself has three major segments. Proximal to the stomach is the **duodenum**, which combines digestive substances from the liver and pancreas; next is the **jejunum**, the primary site of nutrient absorption; finally, the **ileum** absorbs remaining nutrients and moves the remaining matter into the large intestine. The **large intestine** (also called the colon) absorbs water from the waste, which then passes into the **rectum** and out of the body through the **anus**.

Pathologies of the Digestive System

The digestive system is prone to several illnesses of varying severity. Commonly, gastrointestinal distress is caused by an acute infection (bacterial or viral) affecting the lining of the digestive system. A resulting immune response triggers the body, as an adaptive measure, to void the contents of the digestive system in order to purge the infection. Chronic gastrointestinal disorders include **irritable bowel syndrome** (the causes of which are largely unknown) and **Crohn's disease**, an inflammatory bowel disorder with an immune-related etiology.

Practice Questions

10. Where in the digestive tract are most of the nutrients absorbed?
    A) the small intestine
    B) the rectum
    C) the stomach
    D) the large intestine

11. Which of the following initiates the breakdown of carbohydrates?
    A) salivary amylase
    B) stomach acid
    C) bile salts
    D) peristalsis

The Skeletal System

Structure and Function of the Skeletal System

The skeletal system is composed of tissue called **bone** that helps with movement, provides support for organs, and synthesizes blood cells. The outer layer of bone is composed of a matrix made of collagen and minerals that gives bones their strength and rigidity. The matrix is formed from functional units called **osteons** that include layers of compact bone called **lamellae**. The lamellae surround a cavity called the **Haversian canal**, which houses the bone's blood supply. These canals are in turn connected to the **periosteum**, the bone's outermost membrane, by another series of channels called **Volkmann's canals**.

Within osteons are blood cells called **osteoblasts**, mononucleate cells that produce bone tissue. When the bone tissue hardens around these cells, the cells are known as **osteocytes**, and the space they occupy within the bone tissue is known as **lacunae**. The lacunae are connected by a series of channels called **canaliculi**. **Osteoclasts**, a third type of bone cell, are responsible for breaking down bone tissue. They are located on

the surface of bones and help balance the body's calcium levels by degrading bone to release stored calcium. The fourth type of bone cell, **lining cells**, are flatted osteoblasts that protect the bone and also help balance calcium levels.

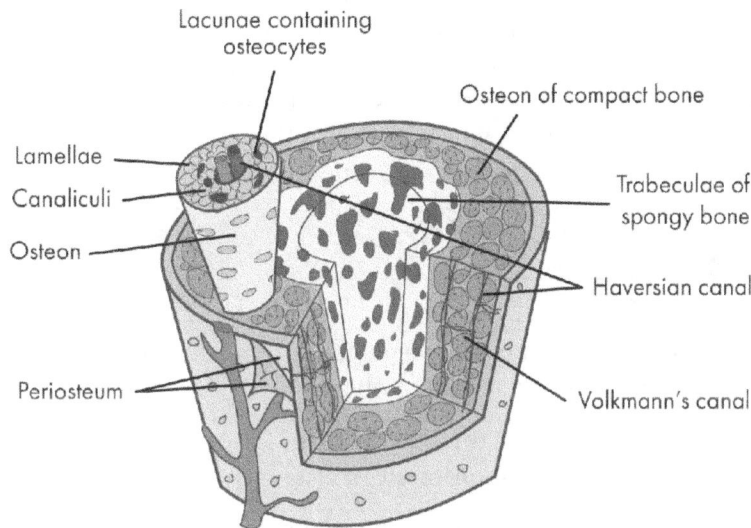

Within the hard outer layer of bone is the spongy layer called **cancellous bone**, which is made up of support structures called **trabeculae**. Within this layer is the bone marrow, which houses cells that produce red blood cells in a process called **hematopoiesis**. Bone marrow also produces many of the lymphocytes that play an important role in the immune system.

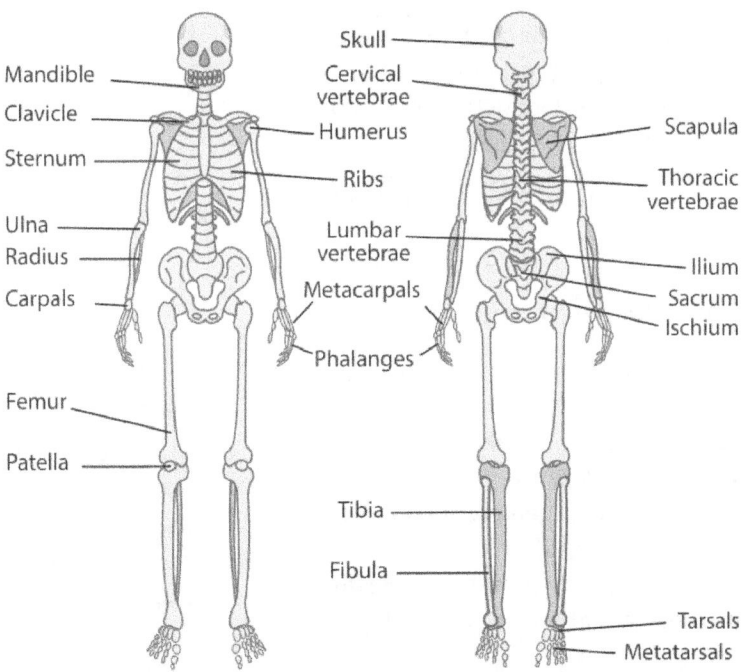

Bones are divided into four main categories. **Long bones**, such as the femur and humerus, are longer than they are wide. **Short bones**, in contrast, are wider than they are long. These include the clavicle

Anatomy and Physiology

and carpals. **Flat bones** are wide and flat, and usually provide protection. Examples of flat bones include the bones of the skull, pelvis, and rib cage. **Irregular bones**, as the name suggests, have an irregular shape that doesn't fit into the other categories. These bones include the vertebrae and bones of the jaw.

Bones are held together (articulated) at **joints** by connective tissue called **ligaments**. Joints can be classified based on the tissue that connects the bone. **Fibrous joints** are connected by dense, collagen-rich fibers, while **cartilaginous joints** are joined by special tissue called **hyaline cartilage**. Cartilage is more flexible than bone but denser than muscles. In addition to joining together bone, it also helps hold open passageways and provides support in structures like the nose and ears. The third type of joint, **synovial joints**, are joined by synovial fluid, which lubricates the joint and allows for movement. Bones are also joined to muscles by connective tissue called **tendons**.

Table 3.2. Types of Synovial Joints

Name	Movement	Found In
Hinge joint	movement through one plane of motion as flexion/extension	elbows, knees, fingers
Ball-and-socket joint	range of motion through multiple planes and rotation about an axis	hips, shoulders
Saddle joint	movement through multiple planes, but cannot rotate about an axis	thumbs
Gliding joint	sliding movement in the plane of the bones' surfaces	vertebrae, small bones in the wrists and ankles
Condyloid joint	movement through two planes as flexion/ extension and abduction/adduction, but cannot rotate about an axis	wrists
Pivot joint	only movement is rotation about an axis	elbows, neck

Pathologies of the Skeletal System

Important pathologies of the skeletal system include **osteoporosis**, which occurs when minerals are leached from the bone, making bones more likely to break. Broken bones can also be caused by **brittle bone disease**, which results from a genetic defect that affects collagen production. Joint pain can be caused by **osteoarthritis**, which is the breakdown of cartilage in joints, and **rheumatoid arthritis**, which is an autoimmune disease that affects synovial membranes.

> **HELPFUL HINT**
>
> Some skeletal muscles, such as the diaphragm and those that control blinking, can be voluntarily controlled but usually operate involuntarily.

Practice Questions

12. Which type of cell is responsible for the degradation of bone tissue?
    A) osteoclasts
    B) osteoblasts
    C) osteocytes
    D) lining cells

13. Which joint allows for the most freedom of movement?
    A) fibrous joints
    B) hinge joints
    C) saddle joints
    D) ball and socket joints

The Muscular System

Types of Muscle

The muscular system is composed of **muscles** that move the body, support bodily functions, and circulate blood. The human body contains three types of muscles. **Skeletal muscles** are voluntarily controlled and attach to the skeleton to allow movement in the body. **Smooth muscles** are involuntary, meaning they cannot be consciously controlled. Smooth muscles are found in many organs and structures, including the esophagus, stomach, intestines, blood vessels, bladder, and bronchi. Finally, **cardiac muscles**, found only in the heart, are the involuntary muscles that contract the heart in order to pump blood through the body.

Muscle Cell Structure

The main structural unit of a muscle is the **sarcomere**. Sarcomeres are composed of a series of **muscle fibers**, which are elongated individual cells that stretch from one end of the muscle to the other. Within each fiber are hundreds of **myofibrils**, long strands within the cells that contain alternating layers of thin filaments made of the protein **actin** and thick filaments made of the protein **myosin**. Each of these proteins plays a role in muscle contraction and relaxation.

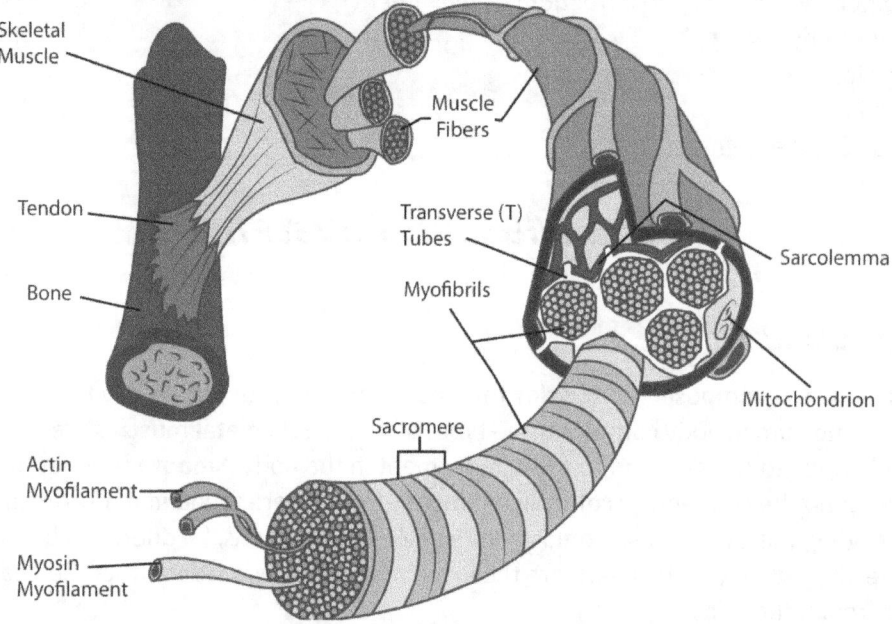

Muscle contraction is explained by the **sliding filament theory**. When the sarcomere is at rest, the thin filaments containing actin are found at both ends of the muscle, while the thick filaments containing myosin are found at the center. Myosin filaments contain "heads," which can attach and detach from actin filaments. The myosin attaches to actin and pulls the thin filaments to the center of the sarcomere, forcing the thin filaments to slide inward and causing the entire sarcomere to shorten, or contract, creating movement. The sarcomere can be broken down into zones that contain certain filaments.

- The Z-line separates the sarcomeres: a single sarcomere is the distance between two Z-lines.

- The A-band is the area of the sarcomere in which thick myosin filaments are found and does not shorten during muscular contraction.

- The I-band is the area in the sarcomere between the thick myosin filaments in which only thin actin filament is found.

- The H-zone is found between the actin filaments and contains only thick myosin filament.

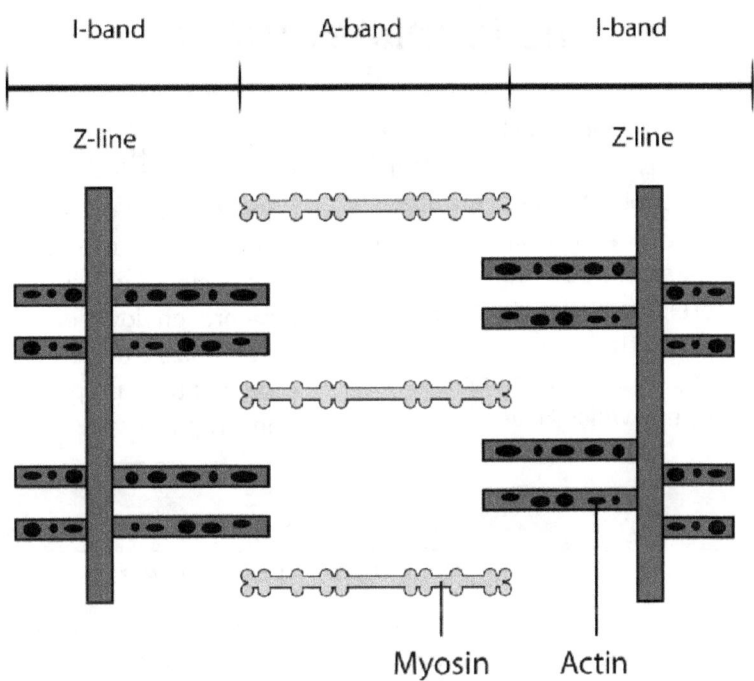

Pathologies of the Muscular System

Injuries to muscle can impede movement and cause pain. When muscle fibers are overstretched, the resulting **muscle strain** can cause pain, stiffness, and bruising. Muscle fibers can also be weakened by diseases, as with **muscular dystrophy** (MD). MD is a genetically inherited condition that results in progressive muscle wasting, which limits movement and can cause respiratory and cardiovascular difficulties.

HELPFUL HINT
Overstretching a ligament is called a *sprain*.

Practice Questions

14. Which type of muscle is responsible for voluntary movement in the body?
    A) cardiac
    B) visceral
    C) smooth
    D) skeletal

15. Which of the following causes a muscle strain?
    A) a lack of available energy
    B) the inability of muscle fibers to contract
    C) detachment of the ligament from the bone
    D) overstretching of muscle fibers

Anatomy and Physiology

The Immune System

The human immune system protects the body against bacteria and viruses that cause disease. The system is composed of two parts. The **innate** system includes nonspecific defenses that work against a wide range of infectious agents. This system includes both physical barriers that keep out foreign particles and organisms along with specific cells that attack invaders that move past barriers. The second part of the immune system is the **adaptive** immune system, which "learns" to respond only to specific invaders.

> **HELPFUL HINT**
>
> Phagocytosis occurs when a cell completely surrounds a particle to form an enclosed vesicle. The particle can then be broken down either for nutrients or to neutralize a threat. Cells in the immune system that use phagocytosis are called macrophages.

Table 3.3. Lines of Defense in the Immune System

1. External barriers	skin, enzymes, mucus, earwax, native bacteria
2. The innate response	inflammation, neutrophils (a white blood cell), antimicrobial peptides, natural killer lymphocytes, interferon
3. The adaptive response	helper T cells, cytotoxic T cells, B cells, memory B cells

The Innate Immune System

The first line of defense in the immune system are barriers to entry. The most prominent is the **skin**, which leaves few openings for an infection-causing agent to enter. Bodily orifices exhibit other methods for preventing infection. The mouth is saturated with native bacteria that dominate the resources in the microenvironment, making it inhospitable to invading bacteria. In addition, enzymes in the mouth create a hostile environment for foreign organisms. The urethra flushes away potentially invasive microorganisms mechanically through the outflow of urine, while the vagina maintains a consistently low pH, deterring potential infections. The eyes and nose constantly produce and flush away tears and **mucus**, which trap pathogens before they can replicate and infect. Similarly, **earwax** serves as an additional barrier to entry.

Pathogens do occasionally breach these barriers and arrive within the body, where they attempt to replicate and cause an infection. When this occurs, the body mounts a number of nonspecific responses. The body's initial response is **inflammation**: infected cells release signaling molecules indicating that an infection has occurred, which causes increased blood flow to the area. This increase in blood flow includes the increased presence of **white blood cells**, also called **leukocytes**. The most common type of leukocyte found at sites of inflammation are **neutrophils**, which engulf and destroy invaders.

Other innate responses include **antimicrobial peptides**, which destroy bacteria by interfering with the functions of their membranes or DNA, and **natural killer lymphocytes**, which respond to virus-infected cells. Because they can recognize damaged cells with the presence of antibodies, they are important in early defense against bacterial infection. In addition, infected cells may release **interferon**, which causes nearby cells to increase their defenses.

Table 3.4. Types of White Blood Cells

Type of Cell	Name of Cell	Role	Innate or Adaptive	Prevalence
Granulocytes	Neutrophil	First responders that quickly migrate to the site of infections to destroy bacterial invaders	Innate	Very common
	Eosinophil	Attack multicellular parasites	Innate	Rare
	Basophil	Large cell responsible for inflammatory reactions, including allergies	Innate	Very rare
Lymphocyte	B cells	Respond to antigens by releasing antibodies	Adaptive	Common
	T cells	Respond to antigens by destroying invaders and infected cells	Adaptive	
	Natural killer cells	Destroy virus-infected cells and tumor cells	Innate and adaptive	
Monocyte	Macrophage	Engulf and destroy microbes, foreign substances, and cancer cells	Innate and adaptive	Rare

The Adaptive Immune System

The adaptive immune system is able to recognize molecules called **antigens** on the surface of pathogens to which the system has previously been exposed. Antigens are displayed on the surface of cells by the **major histocompatibility complex** (MHC), which can display either "self" proteins from their own cells or proteins from pathogens. In an **antigen-presenting cell**, the MHC on the cell's surface displays a particular antigen, which is recognized by **helper T cells**. These cells produce a signal (cytokines) that activates **cytotoxic T cells**, which then destroy any cell that displays the antigen.

> **HELPFUL HINT**
>
> Memory B cells are the underlying mechanisms behind vaccines, which introduce a harmless version of a pathogen into the body to activate the body's adaptive immune response.

The presence of antigens also activates **B cells**, which rapidly multiply to create **plasma cells**, which in turn release **antibodies**. Antibodies will bind only to specific antigens, and in turn result in the destruction of the infected cell. Some interfere directly with the function of the cell, while others draw the attention of macrophages. **Memory B cells** are created during infection. These cells "remember" the antigen that their parent cells responded to, allowing them to respond more quickly if the infection appears again.

Together, T and B cells are known as **lymphocytes**. T cells are produced in the thymus, while B cells mature in bone marrow. These cells circulate through the lymphatic system.

Pathologies of the Immune System

The immune system itself can be pathological. The immune system of individuals with an **autoimmune disease** will attack healthy tissues, as is the case in lupus, psoriasis, and multiple sclerosis. The immune system may also overreact to harmless particles, a condition known as an **allergy**. Some infections will attack the immune system itself. **Human immunodeficiency virus (HIV)** attacks helper T cells, eventually causing **acquired immunodeficiency syndrome (AIDS)**, which allows opportunistic infections to overrun the body.

Practice Questions

16. Which of the following is NOT part of the innate immune system?
    A) interferon
    B) neutrophils
    C) antibodies
    D) natural killer lymphocytes

17. Which of the following is NOT considered a nonspecific defense of the innate immune system?
    A) the skin
    B) inflammation
    C) antimicrobial peptides
    D) antibody production

The Reproductive System

The Male Reproductive System

The male reproductive system produces **sperm**, or male gametes, and passes them to the female reproductive system. Sperm are produced in the **testes** (also called testicles), which are housed externally in a sac-like structure called the **scrotum**. The scrotum contracts and relaxes to move the testes closer or farther from the body. This process keeps the testes at the appropriate temperature for sperm production, which is slightly lower than regular body temperature.

Mature sperm are stored in the **epididymis**. During sexual stimulation, sperm travel from the epididymis through a long, thin tube called the **vas deferens**. Along the way, the sperm is joined by fluids from three glands to form **semen**. The **seminal vesicles** secrete the bulk of the fluid that makes up semen, which is composed of various proteins, sugars, and enzymes. The **prostate** contributes an alkaline fluid that counteracts the acidity of the vaginal tract. Finally, the **Cowper gland** secretes a protein-rich fluid that acts as a lubricant. Semen travels through the **urethra** and exits the body through the **penis**, which becomes rigid during sexual arousal.

The main hormone associated with the male reproductive system is **testosterone**, which is released by the testes (and in the adrenal glands in much smaller amounts). Testosterone is responsible for the development of the male reproductive system and male secondary sexual characteristics, including muscle development and facial hair growth.

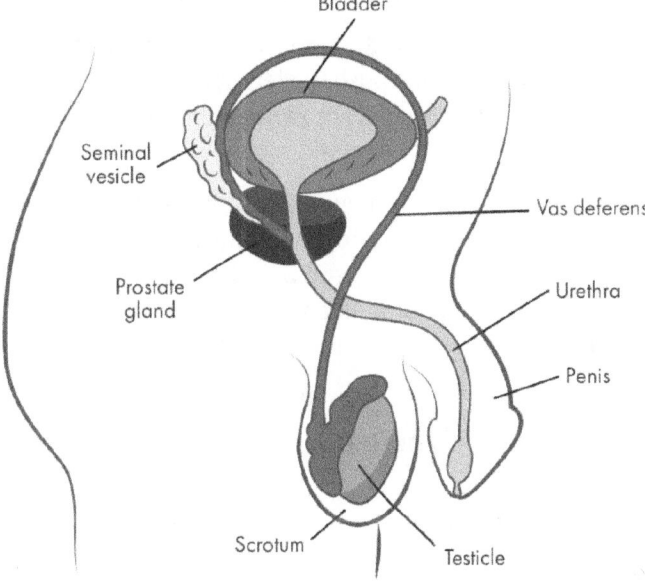

The Female Reproductive System

The female reproductive system produces **eggs**, or female gametes, and gestates the fetus during pregnancy. Eggs are produced in the **ovaries** and travel through the **fallopian tubes** to the **uterus**, which is a muscular organ that houses the fetus during pregnancy. The uterine cavity is lined with a layer of blood-rich tissue called the **endometrium**. If no pregnancy occurs, the endometrium is shed monthly during **menstruation**.

> **QUICK REVIEW**
>
> What type of muscle is most likely found in the myometrium of the uterus?

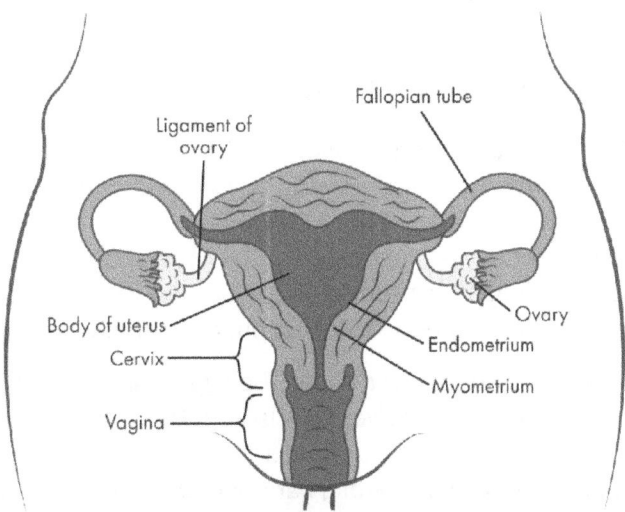

Fertilization occurs when the egg absorbs the sperm; it usually takes place in the fallopian tubes but may happen in the uterus itself. After fertilization the new zygote implants itself in the endometrium,

Anatomy and Physiology

where it will grow and develop over thirty-eight weeks (roughly nine months). During gestation, the developing fetus acquires nutrients and passes waste through the **placenta**. This temporary organ is attached to the wall of the uterus and is connected to the baby by the **umbilical cord**.

When the fetus is mature, powerful muscle contractions occur in the myometrium, the muscular layer next to the endometrium. These contractions push the fetus through an opening called the **cervix** into the vagina, from which it exits the body. The placenta and umbilical cords are also expelled through the vagina shortly after birth.

The female reproductive cycle is controlled by a number of different hormones. Estrogen, produced by the ovaries, stimulates Graafian follicles, which contain immature eggs cells. The pituitary gland then releases luteinizing hormone, which causes the egg to be released into the fallopian tubes during **ovulation**. During pregnancy, estrogen and progesterone are released in high levels to help with fetal growth and to prevent further ovulation.

Practice Questions

18. Which of the following organs transports semen through the penis?
    A) urethra
    B) vas deferens
    C) prostate
    D) seminal vesicles

19. Which of the following organs provides nutrients to a fetus during gestation?
    A) ovary
    B) placenta
    C) uterus
    D) cervix

The Endocrine System

Structure and Function of the Endocrine System

The endocrine system is composed of a network of organs called **glands** that produce signaling chemicals called **hormones**. These hormones are released by glands into the bloodstream and then travel to the other tissues and organs whose functions they regulate. When they reach their target, hormones bond to a specific receptor on cell membranes, which affects the machinery of the cell. Hormones play an important role in regulating almost all bodily functions, including digestion, respiration, sleep, stress, growth, development, reproduction, and immune response.

Much of the action of the endocrine system runs through the **hypothalamus**, which is highly integrated into the nervous system. The hypothalamus receives signals from the brain and in turn will release hormones that regulate both other endocrine organs and important metabolic processes. Other endocrine glands include the pineal, pituitary, thyroid, parathyroid, thymus, and adrenal glands.

Organs from other systems, including the reproductive and digestive systems, can also secrete hormones, and thus are considered part of the endocrine system. The reproductive organs in both males (testes) and females (ovaries and placenta) release important hormones, as do the pancreas, liver, and stomach.

Table 3.5. Endocrine Glands

Gland	Regulates	Hormones Produced
Pineal gland	circadian rhythms (the sleep/wake cycle)	melatonin
Pituitary gland	growth, blood pressure, reabsorption of water by the kidneys, temperature, pain relief, and some reproductive functions related to pregnancy and childbirth	human growth hormone (HGH), thyroid-stimulating hormone (TSH), prolactin (PRL), luteinizing hormone (LH), follicle-stimulating hormone (FSH), oxytocin, antidiuretic hormone (ADH)
Hypothalamus	pituitary function and metabolic processes including body temperature, hunger, thirst, and circadian rhythms	thyrotropin-releasing hormone (TRH), dopamine, growth-hormone-releasing hormone (GHRH), gonadotropin-releasing hormone (GnRH), oxytocin, vasopressin
Thyroid gland	energy use and protein synthesis	thyroxine (T4), triiodothyronine (T3), calcitonin
Parathyroid	calcium and phosphate levels	parathyroid hormone (PTH)
Adrenal glands	"fight or flight" response, regulation of salt and blood volume	epinephrine, norepinephrine, cortisol, androgens
Pancreas	blood sugar levels and metabolism	insulin, glucagon, somatostatin
Testes	maturation of sex organs, secondary sex characteristics	androgens (e.g., testosterone)
Ovaries	maturation of sex organs, secondary sex characteristics, pregnancy, childbirth, and lactation	progesterone, estrogens
Placenta	gestation and childbirth	progesterone, estrogens, human chorionic gonadotropin, human placental lactogen

Pathologies of the Endocrine System

Disruption of hormone production in specific endocrine glands can lead to disease. An inability to produce insulin results in uncontrolled blood glucose levels, a condition called **diabetes**. Over or underactive glands can lead to conditions like **hypothyroidism**, which is characterized by slow metabolism, and hyperparathyroidism, which can lead to osteoporosis. Tumors on endocrine glands can also damage the functioning of a wide variety of bodily systems.

Practice Questions

20. Which gland in the endocrine system is responsible for regulating blood glucose levels?
    A) adrenal
    B) testes
    C) pineal
    D) pancreas

21. Damage to the parathyroid would most likely affect which of the following?
    A) stress levels
    B) bone density
    C) secondary sex characteristics
    D) circadian rhythms

The Integumentary System

The **integumentary system** refers to the skin (the largest organ in the body) and related structures, including the hair and nails. Skin is composed of three layers. The **epidermis** is the outermost layer of the skin. This waterproof layer contains no blood vessels and acts mainly to protect the body. Under the epidermis lies the **dermis**, which consists of dense connective tissue that allows skin to stretch and flex. The dermis is home to blood vessels, glands, and **hair follicles**. The **hypodermis** is a layer of fat below the dermis that stores energy (in the form of fat) and acts as a cushion for the body. The hypodermis is sometimes called the **subcutaneous layer**.

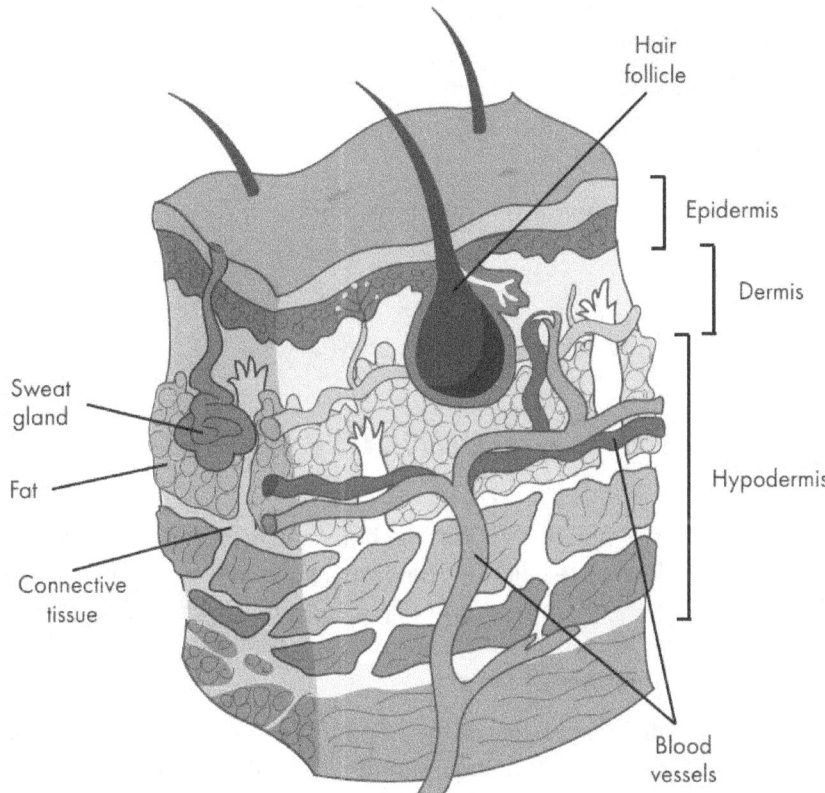

The skin has several important roles. It acts as a barrier to protect the body from injury, the intrusion of foreign particles, and the loss of water and nutrients. It is also important for **thermoregulation**. Blood vessels near the surface of the skin can dilate, allowing for higher blood flow and the release of heat. They can also constrict to reduce the amount of blood that travels near the surface of the skin, which helps conserve heat. The skin also produces vitamin D when exposed to sunlight.

Because the skin covers the whole body, it plays a vital role in allowing organisms to interact with the environment. It is home to nerve endings that sense temperature, pressure, and pain, and it also houses glands that help maintain homeostasis. **Eccrine** glands, which are located primarily in the palms of the hands and soles of the feet (and to a lesser degree in other areas of the body), release the water and salt (NaCl) mixture called **sweat**. These glands help the body maintain the appropriate salt/water balance. Sweat can also contain small amounts of other substances the body needs to expel, including alcohol, lactic acid, and urea.

> **QUICK REVIEW**
>
> Why would flushing—the reddening of the skin caused by dilating blood vessels—be associated with fevers?

Apocrine glands, which are located primarily in the armpit and groin, release an oily substance that contains pheromones. They are also sensitive to adrenaline, and are responsible for most of the sweating that occurs due to stress, fear, anxiety, or pain. Apocrine glands are largely inactive until puberty.

Anatomy and Physiology

Practice Questions

22. Which of the following is NOT a function of the skin?
    A) regulating body temperature
    B) protecting against injury
    C) producing adrenaline
    D) maintaining water/salt balance

23. Which of the following is the outermost layer of the skin?
    A) hypodermis
    B) dermis
    C) epidermis
    D) apocrine

The Genitourinary System

The **urinary system** excretes water and waste from the body and is crucial for maintaining the body's electrolyte balance (the balance of water and salt in the blood). Because many organs function as part of both the reproductive and urinary systems, the two are sometimes referred to collectively as the **genitourinary system**.

> **HELPFUL HINT**
>
> A normal human kidney contains around one million nephrons.

The main organs of the urinary system are the **kidneys**, which filter waste from the blood; maintain the electrolyte balance in the blood; and regulate blood volume, pressure, and pH. The kidneys also function as an endocrine organ and release several important hormones. These include **renin**, which regulates blood pressure, and **calcitriol**, the active form of vitamin D. The kidney is divided into two regions: the **renal cortex**, which is the outermost layer, and the **renal medulla**, which is the inner layer.

The functional unit of the kidney is the **nephron**, which is a series of looping tubes that filter electrolytes, metabolic waste, and other water-soluble waste molecules from the blood. These wastes include **urea**, which is a nitrogenous byproduct of protein catabolism, and **uric acid**, a byproduct of nucleic acid metabolism. Together, these waste products are excreted from the body in **urine**.

Filtration begins in a network of capillaries called a **glomerulus** which is located in the renal cortex of each kidney. This waste is then funneled into **collecting ducts** in the renal medulla. From the collecting ducts, urine passes through the **renal pelvis** and then through two long tubes called **ureters**.

The two ureters drain into the urinary bladder, which holds up to 1,000 milliliters of liquid. The bladder exit is controlled by two sphincters, both of which must open for urine to pass. The internal sphincter is made of smooth involuntary muscle, while the external sphincter can be voluntarily controlled. In males, the external sphincter also closes to prevent movement of seminal fluid into the bladder during sexual activity. (A sphincter is a circular muscle that controls movement of substances through passageways. Sphincters are found throughout the human body, including the bladder, esophagus, and capillaries.)

Urine exits the bladder through the **urethra**. In males, the urethra goes through the penis and also carries semen. In females, the much-shorter urethra ends just above the vaginal opening.

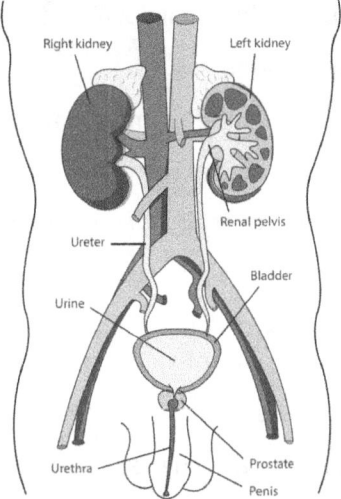

Practice Questions

24. Which of the following is the outermost layer of the kidney?
    A) renal cortex
    B) renal medulla
    C) renal pelvis
    D) nephron

25. Which of the following organs holds urine before it passes into the urethra?
    A) prostate
    B) kidney
    C) ureter
    D) urinary bladder

Answer Key

1. C: Superior means that something is above a reference point.

2. A: The wrist is distal, or further from the trunk, than the elbow.

3. C: The alveoli are sacs found at the terminal end of each bronchiole in the lungs and are the site of gas exchange with the blood.

4. C: Asthma is a negative reaction of the body to otherwise harmless particles.

5, D: These two structures form a junction at the mitral valve.

6. C: The iliac artery receives blood from the aorta to supply blood to the lower body.

7. A: The sinoatrial and atrioventricular nodes electrically stimulate the heart to pump.

8. B: The somatic nervous system controls voluntary actions.

9. B: Dendrites receive information in nerve cells.

10. A: Most nutrients are absorbed by the small intestine.

11. A: Salivary amylase in the mouth begins the breakdown of carbohydrates.

12. A: Osteoclasts break down and absorb bone tissue.

13. D: Ball-and-socket joints allow for the most freedom of movement.

14. D: Skeletal muscles are attached to the skeletal system and are controlled voluntarily.

15. D: A muscle strain is caused by the overstretching of muscle fibers, resulting in tearing of the muscle.

16. C: Antibodies are part of the body's adaptive immune system and only respond to specific pathogens.

17. D: Antibodies are produced by B cells as part of an adaptive immune response.

18. A: The urethra carries semen through the penis.

19. B: The placenta provides nutrients to the growing fetus and also removes waste products.

19. D: The pancreas releases insulin and glucagon, which regulate glucose levels in the blood.

20. B: The parathyroid controls calcium and phosphate levels, which are maintained by producing and reabsorbing bone tissue.

21. C: The skin does not produce adrenaline. (Adrenaline is produced and released by the adrenal glands.)

22. C: The epidermis is the outermost layer of the skin. It is waterproof and does not contain any blood vessels.

23. A: The outermost layer of the kidney is the renal cortex.

24. D: The urinary bladder holds urine before it passes to the urethra to be excreted.

Biology

Biological Macromolecules

There are four basic biological macromolecules that are common between all organisms: carbohydrates, lipids, nucleic acids, and proteins. These molecules make life possible by performing basic cellular functions.

Macromolecules are **polymers**, which are large molecules comprised of smaller molecules called **monomers**. The monomers are joined together in an endothermic (energy requiring) dehydration reaction, so-called because it releases a molecule of water. Conversely, the bonds in polymers can be broken by an exothermic (energy-releasing) reaction that requires water.

Carbohydrates

Carbohydrates, commonly known as sugars, are made up of carbon, hydrogen, and oxygen. The monomers of carbohydrates, called **monosaccharides**, have these elements in the ratio $C_nH_{2n}O_n$. Common monosaccharides include glucose and fructose.

Monosaccharides bond together to build larger carbohydrate molecules. Two monosaccharides bond together to form **disaccharides** such as sucrose and lactose. **Oligosaccharides** are formed when small numbers of monosaccharies (usually between two and ten) bond together, and **polysaccharides** can include hundreds or even thousands of monosaccharides.

Carbohydrates are often taken into the body through ingestion of food and serve a number of purposes, acting as:

- fuel sources (glycogen, amylose)
- means of communication between cells (glycoproteins)
- cell structure support (cellulose, chitin)

Carbohydrates are broken down to their constituent parts for fuel and other biological functions. Inability to process sugars can lead to health issues; for example, inability to break down lactose (often due to problems with the enzyme **lactase**, which serves this function) leads to lactose intolerance, and problems with insulin not working properly in the breakdown of sugars can lead to diabetes.

Lipids

Lipids, commonly known as fats, are composed mainly of hydrogen and carbon. They serve a number of functions depending on their particular structure: they make up the outer structure of cells, and can act as fuel, as steroids, and as hormones. Lipids are hydrophobic, meaning they repel water.

Cholesterol is one example of a lipid, and is essential for normal functioning, although excessive accumulation can cause inflammation issues and high blood pressure. There are two types of cholesterol: **high-density lipoprotein** (**HDL**) and **low-density lipoprotein** (**LDL**), with HDL commonly referred to as "good" cholesterol and LDL as "bad" cholesterol, as high levels of LDL in particular can cause health problems.

Proteins

Proteins serve an incredibly wide variety of purposes within the body. As enzymes, they play key roles in important processes like DNA replication, cellular division, and cellular metabolism. Structural proteins provide rigidity to cartilage, hair, nails, and the cytoskeletons (the network of molecules that holds the parts of a cell in place). They are also involved in communication between cells and in the transportation of molecules.

Proteins are composed of individual **amino acids**, each of which has an amino group and carboxylic acid group, along with other side groups. Amino acids are joined together by **peptide bonds** to form polypeptides. There are twenty amino acids, and the order of the amino acids in the polypeptide determines the shape and function of the molecule.

Nucleic Acids

Nucleic acids store hereditary information and are composed of monomers called **nucleotides**. Each nucleotide includes a sugar, a phosphate group, and a nitrogenous base.

Cytosine C   **Thymine** T   **Adenine** A   **Guanine** G

pyrimidine bases   purine bases

There are two types of nucleic acids. **Deoxyribonucleic acid** (**DNA**) contains the genetic instructions to produce proteins. It is composed of two strings of nucleotides wound into a double helix shape. The backbone of the helix is made from the nucleotide's sugar (deoxyribose) and phosphate groups. The "rungs" of the ladder are made from one of four nitrogenous bases: adenine, thymine, cytosine, and guanine. These bases bond together in specific pairs: adenine with thymine and cytosine with guanine.

Ribonucleic acid (**RNA**) transcribes information from DNA and plays several vital roles in the replication of DNA and the manufacturing of proteins. RNA nucleotides contain a sugar (ribose), a phosphate group, and one of four nitrogenous bases: adenine, uracil, cytosine, and guanine. It is usually found as a single stranded molecule.

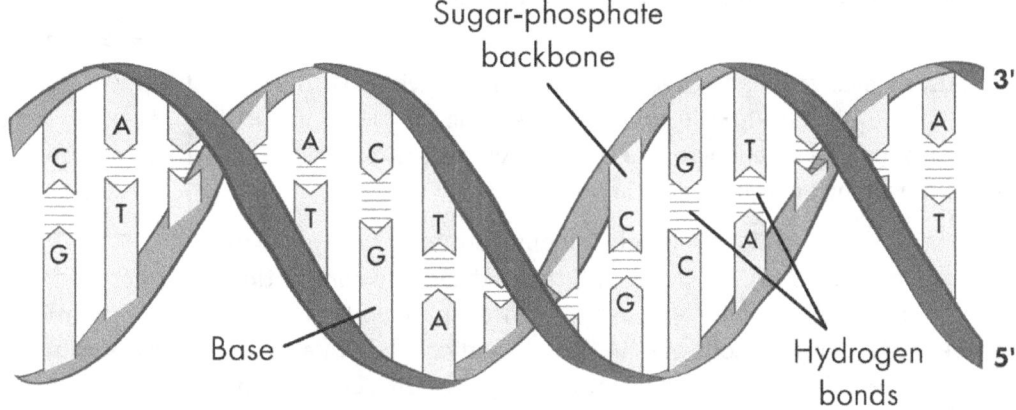

The Structure and Role of DNA

DNA stores information by coding for proteins using blocks of three nucleotides called **codons**. Each codon codes for a specific amino acid; together, all the codons needed to make a specific protein are called a **gene**. In addition to codons for specific amino acids, there are also codons that signal "start" and "stop."

The production of a protein starts with **transcription**. During transcription, the two sides of the DNA helix unwind and a complementary strand of messenger RNA (mRNA) is manufactured using the DNA as a template.

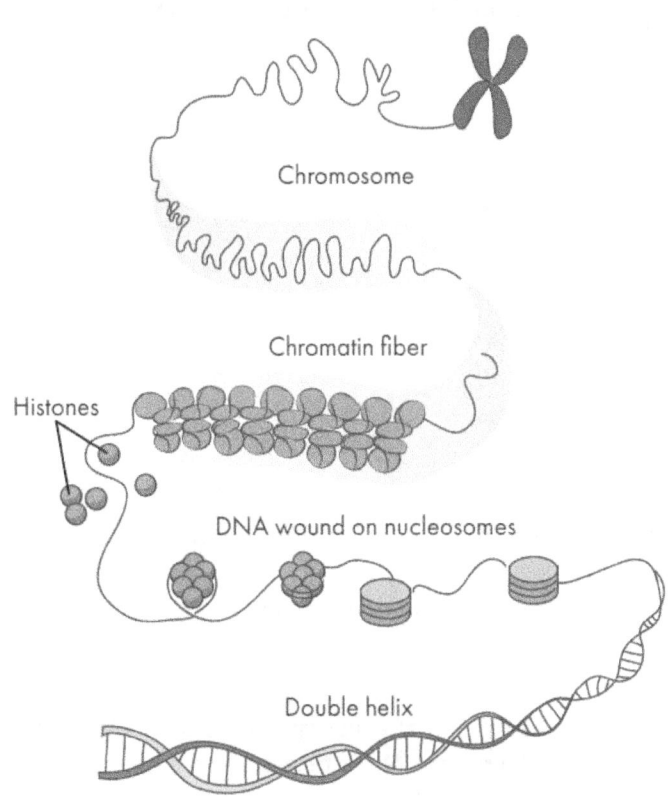

Biology

This mRNA then travels outside the nucleus where it is "read" by a ribosome during **translation**. Each codon on the mRNA is matched to an **anti-codon** on a strand of tRNA, which carries a specific amino acid. The amino acids bond as they are lined up next to each other, forming a polypeptide.

A **mutation** causes a change in the sequence of nucleotides within DNA. For example, the codon GAC codes for the amino acid aspartic acid. However, if the cytosine is swapped for an adenine, the codon now reads GAA, which corresponds to the amino acid glutamic acid.

> **QUICK REVIEW**
>
> How might a mutation in a single codon affect the finished protein?

When it is not being transcribed, DNA is tightly wound around proteins called **histones** to create **nucleosomes**, which are in turn packaged into **chromatin**. The structure of chromatin allows large amounts of DNA to be stored in a very small space and helps regulate transcription by controlling access to specific sections of DNA. Tightly folding the DNA also helps prevent damage to the genetic code. Chromatin is further bundled into packages of DNA called **chromosomes**. During cell division, DNA is replicated to create two identical copies of each chromosome called **chromatids**.

Practice Questions

1. Which of the following is NOT an amino acid found in DNA?
    A) adenine
    B) guanine
    C) uracil
    D) thymine

2. Which of the following processes uses the information stored in RNA to produce a protein?
    A) replication
    B) translation
    C) transcription
    D) mutation

3. Which of the following is a monomer used to build carbohydrates?
    A) glucose
    B) thymine
    C) aspartic acid
    D) histone

The Cell

A **cell** is the smallest unit of life that can reproduce on its own. Unicellular organisms, such as amoebae, are made up of only one cell, while multicellular organisms are composed of many cells. Cells consist of many different parts that work together to maintain the life of the cell.

Cell Membranes

The outer surface of human cells is made up of a **plasma membrane**, which gives the cell its shape. This membrane is primarily composed of a **phospholipid bilayer**, which itself is made up of two layers of lipids facing in opposing directions. This functions to separate the inner cellular environment from the **extracellular space**, the space between cells.

Molecules travel through the cell membrane using a number of different methods. During **diffusion**, molecules pass through the membrane from areas of high to low concentration. (When that molecule is water, the process is called **osmosis**.) **Facilitated diffusion** occurs with the assistance of proteins embedded in the membrane. Diffusion is known as **passive transport** because it does not require energy.

During **active transport**, proteins in the membrane use energy (in the form of ATP) to move molecules across the membrane. Usually these molecules are large or are being moved against their concentration gradient (from areas of low to high concentration).

Cell Organelles

Within the cell, specialized parts known as **organelles** serve individual functions to support the cell. The inside of the cell (excluding the nucleus) is the **cytoplasm**, which includes both organelles and **cytosol**, a fluid that aids in molecular transport and reactions.

The function of individual organelles can be compared to the functions of components in a city. The "power plant" for the cell is its mitochondria, which produce energy for the cell in the form of **adenosine triphosphate** (**ATP**). This process is known as **cellular respiration**, as it requires oxygen that is taken in from the lungs and supplied in blood. Byproducts of cellular respiration are water and carbon dioxide, the latter of which is transported into blood and then to the lungs, where it is exhaled.

The "city hall" of the cell is the cell **nucleus**, which is where the cell's "instructions" governing its functions originate. The nucleus contains the cell's DNA and is surrounded by a **nuclear membrane**. Only eukaryotic cells have nuclei; prokaryotic nucleic acids are not contained with a membrane-bound organelle.

The transporting "railway" function is largely served by **endoplasmic reticulum**. Proteins and lipids travel along endoplasmic reticulum as they are constructed and transported within the cell. There are two types of endoplasmic reticulum, **smooth** and **rough**, which are distinguished by the fact that the latter is embedded with **ribosomes**. Also, smooth endoplasmic reticulum are associated with the production and transport of lipids, whereas rough endoplasmic reticulum are associated with the production and transport of proteins. Ribosomes themselves are sites of protein production; here, molecules produced from the nucleus-encoding proteins guide the assembly of proteins from amino acids.

The **Golgi apparatus** is another organelle involved in protein synthesis and transport. After a new protein is synthesized at the ribosome and travels along the endoplasmic reticulum, the Golgi apparatus packages it into a **vesicle** (essentially a plasma membrane "bubble"), which can then be transported within the cell or secreted outside of the cell, as needed.

Plant cells include a number of structures not found in animal cells. These include the **cell wall**, which provides the cell with a hard outer structure, and **chloroplasts**, where photosynthesis occurs. During

photosynthesis, plants store energy from sunlight as sugars, which serve as the main source of energy for cell functions.

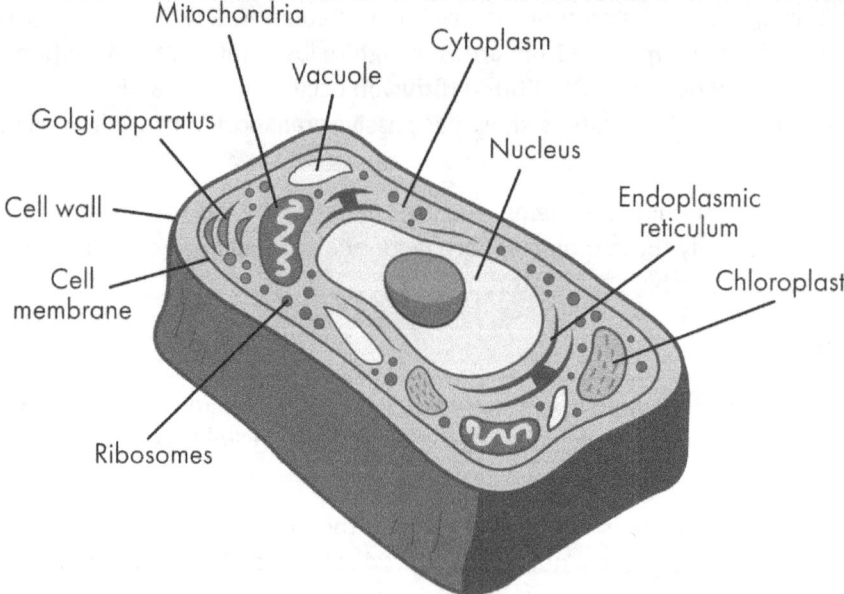

The Cell Cycle

From the very earliest moments of life throughout adulthood, cell division is a critical function of cell biology. The rate of division differs between cell types; hair and skin cells divide relatively rapidly (which is why chemotherapy drugs, which target rapidly dividing cells in an effort to destroy cancerous cells, often cause hair loss), whereas liver cells rarely divide, except in response to injury. Regardless of cell type (with the exception of reproductive cells), the process of cell division follows consistent stages, which make up the **cell cycle**.

The cell cycle is made up of five stages. Cells at rest, which are not dividing, are considered to be at the G_0 (**growth phase 0**) stage of the cell cycle. Once cell division is triggered (for example, by extracellular signals in response to nearby damage, requiring new cells to replace the damaged cells), cells enter stage G_1. In this stage, the organelles of the soon-to-be-dividing cell are duplicated, in order to support both daughter cells upon division. Similarly, in the next stage, **S** (**DNA synthesis**) **phase**, the genetic material of the cell (DNA) is duplicated, to ensure that each cell has the full complement of genetic instructions. Additional growth and protein production occurs in the subsequent stage, G_2 **phase**.

G_1, S, and G_2 are collectively known as **interphase**, in which the cell is growing and preparing to divide; the subsequent stages in which the cell is actively dividing are stages of **mitosis**. The first mitotic stage is **prophase**, in which the newly replicated DNA condenses into chromosomes. These chromosomes are in pairs (humans have twenty-three pairs of chromosomes), with each pair joined together at the **centromere**.

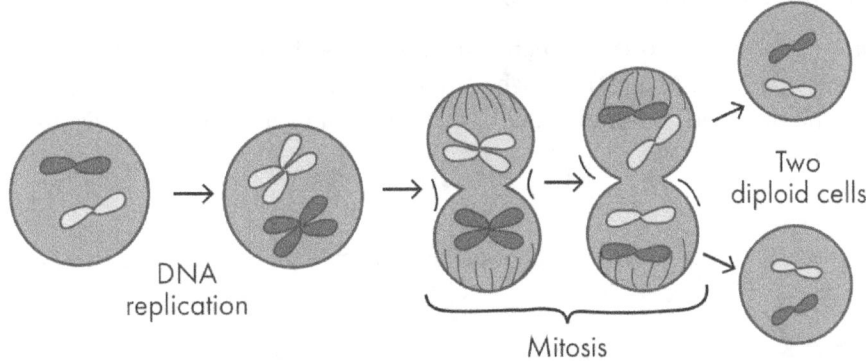

Next, in **prometaphase**, the nuclear membrane breaks down. **Kinetochores** form on chromosomes, which are proteins that attach to kinetochore **microtubules** (cellular filaments) anchored at opposite ends of the cell. In **metaphase**, the chromosomes align along the center of the cell, perpendicular to the poles anchoring the microtubules. The alignment is such that one of each chromosome duplicates is attached to each pole by these microtubules.

In **anaphase**, the microtubules pull the duplicates apart from each other toward each of the poles. In the final stage of mitosis, **telophase**, nuclei reform in each pole of the cell, and cellular filaments contract. The process of **cytokinesis** divides the cell into two daughter cells, both with a full complement of genetic material and organelles.

Following mitosis, both daughter cells return to the G_1 phase, either to begin the process of division once again or to rest without dividing (G_0).

The process of producing sex cells (**gametes**: **ovum** for women and **spermatozoa** for men) is similar to mitosis, except that it produces cells with only half the normal number of chromosomes. Thus, when two sex cells fuse, the resulting **zygote** has the proper amount of chromosomes (and genetic information from both parents). This process is known as **meiosis**.

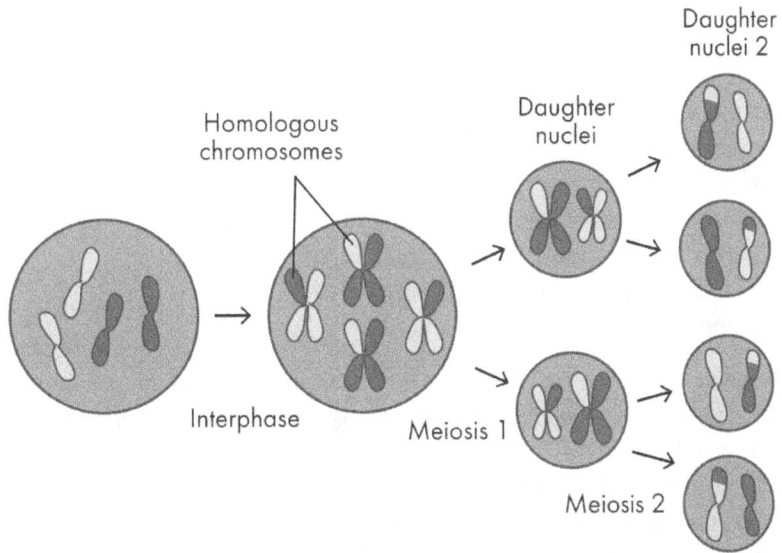

In the prophase of meiosis, chromosome pairs align next to each other. At this stage, transfer of genetic material can occur between members of each pair, in a process known as **homologous recombination**, which can increase the genetic diversity of offspring.

In meiotic metaphase, these chromosomes align as pairs in the center of the cell, and the chromosomes are separated during anaphase. As a result, each gamete cell ends up with one copy of each chromosome pair, and thus one half of the genetic complement necessary for the zygote.

Practice Questions

4. Cellular respiration produces which of the following molecules?
   A) oxygen
   B) DNA
   C) ATP
   D) glucose

5. Which of the following houses the cell's DNA?
   A) rough endoplasmic reticulum
   B) smooth endoplasmic reticulum
   C) mitochondrion
   D) nucleus

6. Which of the following processes creates daughter cells with half the number of chromosomes contained in somatic (body) cells?
   A) mitosis
   B) meiosis
   C) recombination
   D) the cell cycle

Genetics

Heredity

When organisms reproduce, **genetic** information is passed to the next generation through DNA. Within DNA are blocks of nucleotides called genes, each of which contains the code needed to produce a specific protein. Genes are responsible for **traits**, or characteristics, in organisms such as eye color, height, and flower color. The sequence of nucleotides in DNA is called an organism's **genotype**, while the resulting physical traits are the organism's **phenotype**.

> **HELPFUL HINT**
>
> Many of the rules of genetics were discovered by Gregor Mendel, a nineteenth century abbot who used pea plants to show how traits are passed down through generations.

Different versions of the same gene (e.g., one that codes for blue eyes and one for green eyes) are called **alleles**. During sexual reproduction, the child receives two alleles of each gene—one each on the mother's chromosomes and the father's chromosomes. These alleles can be **homozygous** (identical) or **heterozygous** (different). If the organism is heterozygous for a particular gene, which allele is expressed is determined by which alleles are dominant and/or recessive. According to the rules of Mendelian heredity, **dominant** alleles will always be expressed, while **recessive** alleles are only expressed if the organism has no dominant alleles for that gene.

The genotype, and resulting phenotype, of sexually reproducing organisms can be tracked using Punnett squares, which show the alleles of the **parent generation** on each of two axes. (Note that dominant alleles are always depicted using capital letters while recessive alleles are written in lower case.) The possible phenotype of the resulting offspring, called the **F1 generation**, are then shown in the body of the square. The squares do not show the phenotypes of any one offspring; instead, they show the ratio of phenotypes found across the generation. In Figure 4.8, two heterozygous parents for trait *R* are mated, resulting in a ratio of 1:2:1 for homozygous dominant, heterozygous, and homozygous recessive. Note that this creates a 3:1 ratio of dominant to recessive phenotypes.

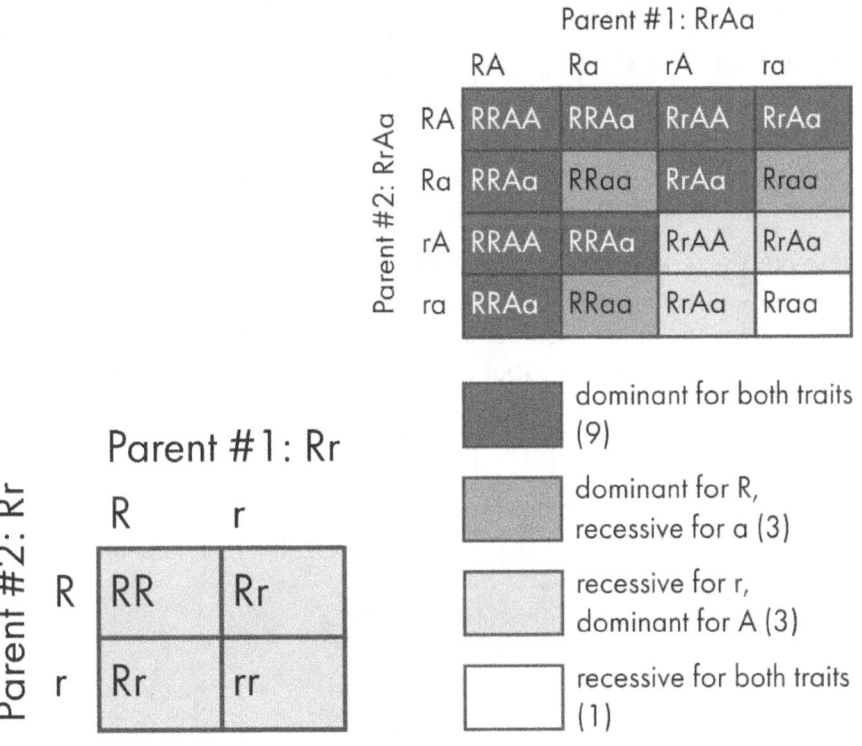

Similarly, crossing two parents that are heterozygous for two traits (dihybrids) results in a phenotypic ratio of 9:3:3:1, as shown in Figure 4.9. This ratio is known as the **dihybrid ratio**.

Non-Mendelian inheritance describes patterns in inheritance that do not follow the ratios described above. The patterns can occur for a number of reasons. Alleles might show **incomplete dominance**, where one allele is not fully expressed over the other, resulting in a third phenotype (for example, a red flower and white flower cross to create a pink flower). Alleles can also be **codominant**, meaning both are fully expressed (such as the AB blood type).

> **HELPFUL HINT**
>
> When the F1 generation is mated together, the resulting offspring are called the F2 generation.

The expression of genes can also be regulated by mechanisms other than the dominant/recessive relationship. For example, some genes may inhibit the expression of other genes, a process called **epistasis**. The environment can also impact gene expression. For example, organisms with the same genotype may grow to different sizes depending on the nutrients available to them.

Biology

When a person's genetic code is damaged, that organism may have a **genetic disorder**. For example, cystic fibrosis, which causes difficulty with basic bodily functions such as breathing and eating, results from damage to the gene that codes for a protein called CFTR. Down syndrome, which causes developmental delays, occurs when a person has three copies of chromosome 21 (meaning they received two copies from a parent as a result of an error in meiosis).

Natural Selection and Evolution

Genes are not static. Over time, **mutations**, or changes in the genetic code, occur that can affect an organism's ability to survive. Harmful mutations will appear less often in a population or be removed entirely because those organisms will be less likely to reproduce (and thus will not pass on that trait). Beneficial mutations may help an organism reproduce, and thus that trait will appear more often. Over time, this process, called **natural selection**, results in the evolution of new species. The theory of evolution was developed by naturalist Charles Darwin based in part on his observations of finches on the Galapagos Islands. These finches had a variety of beak shapes and sizes that allowed them to coexist by using different food sources.

> **QUICK REVIEW**
> Why might a harmful mutation continue to exist in a population?

As a result of these processes, all organisms share a distant evolutionary predecessor. As evolution progressed, species subsequently split off as different branches of the phylogenetic (evolutionary) tree of species diversity, leading to the complexity of life seen today. For example, humans share a recent evolutionary ancestor with other primates (but did not evolve directly from any of these species).

Practice Questions

7. If a plant that is homozygous dominant (T) for a trait is crossed with a plant that is homozygous recessive (t) for the same trait, what will be the phenotype of the offspring if the trait follows mendelian patterns of inheritance?
    A) All of offspring will show the dominant phenotype.
    B) All offspring will show the recessive phenotype.
    C) Half the offspring will show the dominant trait, and the other half will show the recessive phenotype.
    D) All the offspring will show a mix of the dominant and recessive phenotypes.

8. Which of the following mutations would most likely be passed on to an organism's offspring?
    A) a mutation that prevents the production of functioning sperm cells
    B) a mutation that causes the deterioration of nerve cells in mature adults
    C) a mutation that does not cause any changes to the organism's phenotype
    D) a mutation that limits the growth of bone cell sin children

Answer Key

1. C: Uracil is found only in RNA.

2. B: Translation is the process of matching codons in RNA to the correct anti-codon to manufacture a protein.

3. A: Glucose is a monosaccharide that can be used to build larger polysaccharides.

4. C: Cellular respiration uses glucose and oxygen to produce ATP.

5. D: Smooth and rough endoplasmic reticula process and transport lipids and proteins, and mitochondria produce the cell's chemical energy.

6. B: Meiosis produces sex cells, which have half the number of chromosomes that somatic cells contain.

7. A: Because each offspring will inherit the dominant allele, all the offspring will show the dominant phenotype. The offspring would only show a mix of the two phenotypes if they did not follow Mendelian inheritance patterns.

8. B: Because this mutation presents in older adults who have likely already reproduced, it is likely to have been passed on to the next generation. Mutations that affect reproduction and children are much less likely to be passed on. A mutation that causes no changes in phenotype may either disappear or spread as a result of random fluctuations in the gene pool.

Chemistry

Properties of Atoms

An atom is defined as the smallest constituent unit of an element that still retains all of the original properties of the element, and all matter is composed of atoms. Atoms are not irreducible, however, and may be broken into further components: protons, neutrons, and electrons. All atomic nuclei are comprised of positively charged **protons** and neutrally charged **neutrons**, meaning nuclei have an overall positive charge.

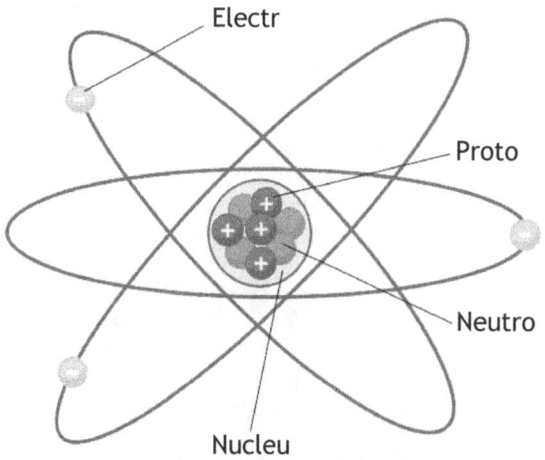

HELPFUL HINT

The attractive and repulsive forces in an atom follow the universal law that "like charges repel and opposite charges

Negatively charged electrons orbit the nucleus in orbitals, with the orbitals closer to the nucleus having less energy than those farther away. Thus, overall atomic charge is determined by the number of positively charged protons and negatively charged electrons in an atom.

Every atom of an element has the same number of protons, which is that element's atomic number. Elements are arranged on the Periodic Table of the Elements by their atomic number which increases from top to bottom and left to right on the table. Hydrogen, the first element on the periodic table, has one proton while helium, the second element, has two, and so on.

Along with atomic charge, atoms have measurable mass. Protons and neutrons are significantly more massive than electrons (about 1,800 times), so the mass of electrons is not considered when calculating the mass of an atom. Thus, an element's **mass number** is the number of protons and neutrons present in its atoms. The number of neutrons in an atom can be found by subtracting the atomic number from the mass number.

HELPFUL HINT

atomic number = number of protons

mass number = number of protons + number of neutrons

atomic mass = average mass of all isotopes

While atoms of the same element have the same number of protons, their number of neutrons may vary. Atoms which differ in their number of neutrons but have equal numbers of protons are **isotopes** of the same element.

When writing the atomic symbol of an element, isotopes are differentiated by writing the mass number in the upper left-hand corner of the symbol. The atomic symbol for ordinary hydrogen is written as $_1H$, to signify that it has no neutrons and 1 proton, while deuterium, which is a hydrogen isotope with 1 neutron, is written as $_2H$.

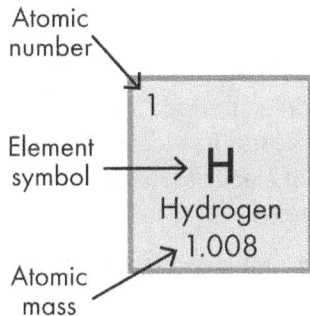

The **atomic mass** of an atom, which is different from the mass number, is the average mass of all known isotopes of an element. For each element on the Periodic Table, the atomic number is listed above the symbol of the element and the atomic mass (measured in atomic mass units, or AMU) is listed underneath the symbol.

Atoms may lose or gain electrons, creating charged particles called **ions**. Ions are called **cations** if they are positively charged (due to the loss of electrons) or **anions** if they are negatively charged (due to the gaining of electrons). Ionic charges are denoted by adding a plus or minus sign onto the elemental symbol; for example, a sodium ion with a charge of +1 would be written as Na_+.

Ions may be composed of two or more atoms known as molecular ions or **polyatomic ions**. The overall charge of a polyatomic ion is equal to the sum of the charges of all constituent atoms.

Table 5.1. Common Polyatomic Ions	
NH^{4+}	ammonium
H_3O^+	hydronium
PO_4^{3-}	phosphate
SO_4^{2-}	sulfate
MnO_4^{2-}	manganate
OH^-	hydroxide
CN^-	cyanide

Table 5.1. Common Polyatomic Ions	
CO_3^{2-}	carbonate
HCO_3^{1-}	hydrogen carbonate
ClO^{2-}	chlorite

The Periodic Table of the Elements

There are many useful physical and chemical patterns represented in the Periodic Table of the Elements. The periodic table is organized into rows called **periods** and columns called **groups**. The position of an element's symbol on the periodic table indicates its electron configuration. The elements in each group on the table all contain the same amount of electrons in their valence shell, which results in all elements in a group having similar chemical properties.

The majority of the elements in the periodic table are metals. **Metals** have the following properties:

- They are ductile and malleable.
- They conduct electricity.
- They can form alloys.
- They are thermally conductive.
- They are hard, opaque, and shiny.
- With the exception of mercury, they are solids.

Solid metals usually consist of tightly packed atoms, resulting in fairly high densities. Metals begin on the left side of the periodic table and span across the middle of the table, almost all the way to the right side. Examples of metals include gold (Au), tin (Sn), and lead (Pb).

Nonmetals are elements that do not conduct electricity and tend to be more volatile than metals. They can be solids, liquids, or gases. The nonmetals are located on the right side of the periodic table. Examples of nonmetals include sulfur (S), hydrogen (H), and oxygen (O).

Metalloids, or semimetals, are elements that possess both metal and nonmetal characteristics. For example, some metalloids are shiny but do not conduct electricity well. Many metalloids are semiconductors. Metalloids are located between the metals and nonmetals on the periodic table. Some examples of metalloids are boron (B), silicon (Si), and arsenic (As).

Specific names are given to certain groups on the periodic table. Group 1 elements (belonging to the leftmost column) are known as the **alkali metals** and are characterized by the fact that they are very unstable and react violently with water. Other notably reactive elements are in Group 17, the **halogens**. In contrast to both of these groups, Group 18 contains the **noble gases**, which are inert and very non-reactive because they have a full outer shell of electrons.

There are two periods below and separated from the main periodic table. These are called **lanthanides** and **actinides**. They are set apart from the other elements for two reasons: first, to consolidate the periodic table, and second, because they are more complicated chemically than the rest of the elements—which means that they do not follow any of the trends outlined below.

The periodic table is organized so that elements show trends across periods and groups. Some of these trends are summarized below.

Atomic Number: The atomic number (equal to the number of protons) of an element increases from left to right and top to bottom on the Periodic Table of the Elements. This means that hydrogen, with the lowest atomic number, is located at the upper left corner of the table.

Atomic Radius: Atomic radius (the distance from the center of the atom to its outermost electron shell) increases from right to left and top to bottom on the periodic table, with the largest elements residing in the lower left corner.

Electron Affinity: An atom's electron affinity describes the amount of energy released or gained when an electron is added to the atom. On the periodic table, electron affinity increases from left to right and bottom to top, with the highest electron affinities belonging to elements residing in the upper right corner.

Electronegativity: Electronegativity measures how easily an atom can attract electrons and form chemical bonds. In general, electronegativity increases from left to right and bottom to top on the Periodic Table of the Elements, with fluorine being the most electronegative element. Electronegativity decreases from top to bottom of a group on the periodic table because of the increasing atomic radius, which corresponds with a greater distance between the electron orbital shells. One notable exception to these electronegativity trends is Group 18, the noble gases, since they possess a complete valence shell in their ground state and generally do not attract electrons.

Ionization Energy: The ionization energy of an element is defined as the energy necessary to remove an electron from a neutral atom in its gaseous phase. In other words, the lower this energy is, the more likely an atom is to lose an electron and become a cation. Ionization energies increase from left to right and bottom to top on the periodic table, meaning that the lowest ionization energies are in the lower left corner and the highest are in the upper right corner. This is because elements to the right on the periodic table are unlikely to lose electrons and become cations since their outer valence shells are nearly full.

Electron Configuration

An atom's **electron configuration**—the location of its electrons—influences its physical and chemical properties, including boiling point, conductivity, and its tendency to engage in chemical reactions (also called the atom's stability). The chemical reactivity of an atom is determined by the electrons in the outermost shell, as they are first to interact with neighboring atoms.

Conventionally, electrons are depicted as orbiting a nucleus in defined pathways, much like a planet orbits the sun. In reality, electrons move in clouds surrounding the nucleus known as **orbitals**. Each orbital in an atom holds two electrons.

Orbitals are grouped into four types of **subshells** labeled with the letters s, p, d, and f. Each subshell has a specific number of orbitals:

- s has 1 orbital and holds $1 \times 2 = 2$ electrons
- p has 3 orbitals and holds $3 \times 2 = 6$ electrons
- d has 5 orbitals and holds $5 \times 2 = 10$ electrons
- f has 7 orbitals and holds $7 \times 2 = 14$ electrons

The orbitals in each type of subshell have a particular shape. For example, the s subshell is spherical, while the p subshell is shaped like a bow tie.

Subshells are further grouped into **shells**, which are labeled with integers (1, 2, 3, ...). The shell numbered 1 is closest to the nucleus, and the energy of the electrons in shells increases the further the shell is from the nucleus.

> **HELPFUL HINT**
>
> Electronegativity and ionization energy follow the same periodic trends. These two properties are simply different ways of describing the same basic property: the strength with which an atom holds electrons.

> **HELPFUL HINT**
>
> You can use the periodic table to remember the order in which orbitals are filled: start at the upper left corner and move from left to right, then move down to the next row.

The location of a electron is described by its shell number and subshell letter, with the number of electrons in that orbital given as a superscript. The one electron in hydrogen, for example, is written as $1s^1$.

The orbitals for the first four shells are described in the table below.

Table 5.2. Electron Configuration Notation

Shell	Subshell	No. of Orbitals	No. of Electrons in Subshell	Notation for Full Subshell
1	s	1	2	$1s^2$
2	s	1	2	$2s^2$
2	p	3	6	$2p^6$
3	s	1	2	$3s^2$
3	p	3	6	$3p^6$

Table 5.2. Electron Configuration Notation

Shell	Subshell	No. of Orbitals	No. of Electrons in Subshell	Notation for Full Subshell
	d	5	10	$3d10$
4	s	1	2	$4s2$
	p	3	6	$4p6$
	d	5	10	$4d10$
	f	7	14	$4f14$

Electrons fill orbitals in order of increasing energy, meaning they fill orbitals close to the nucleus before filling in outer orbitals. The order in which orbitals are filled is shown in Figure 5.4.

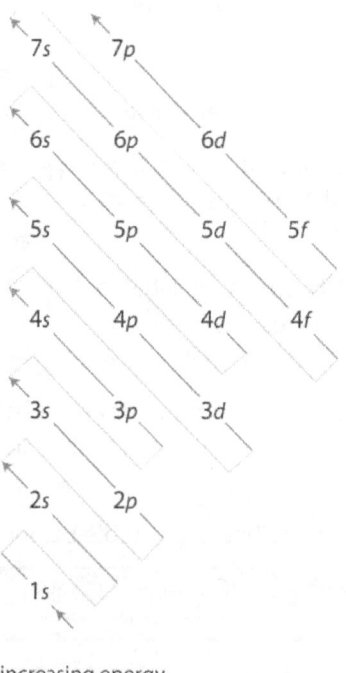

increasing energy

1s 2s 2p 3s 3p 4s 3d 4p 5s 4d 5p 6s ...

The electrons in an atom's outermost shell are its **valence electrons**. Most elements require eight electrons to fill their outermost shell (2 in s and 6 in p). So, elements with six or seven valence electrons are likely to gain electrons (and become cations). Conversely, elements with one or two electrons are very likely to lose electrons (and become anions). Elements with exactly eight electrons (the noble gases), are almost completely unreactive.

The electron configuration of each element correlates to its position on the periodic table: Group 1 and Group 2 (defined as the **s-block**) have valence electrons in s-orbitals. Elements in Groups 13 to 18 (defined as the **p-block**) have valence electrons in their p-orbitals. These groups (with the exception of the noble gases) are very reactive.

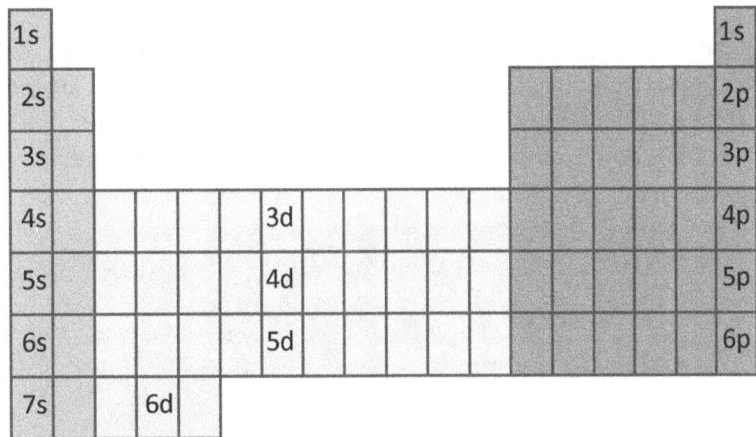

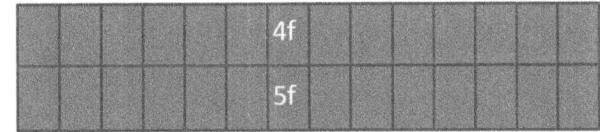

Group 3 through Group 12 elements (defined as the **d-block**) have valence electrons in d-orbitals. The lanthanides and actinides have valence electrons in their f-orbitals (and are called the **f-block**). The properties of these elements are less predictable because atoms' d and f orbitals do not fill in a straightforward order.

Practice Questions

1. Rank the following in order of increasing atomic radius: xenon (Xe), barium (Ba), cesium (Cs).
    A) $Xe < Cs < Ba$
    B) $CS < Xe < Ba$
    C) $Ba < CS < Xe$
    D) $Xe < Ba < Cs$

2. What is the electron configuration of ground state neutral magnesium (Mg)?
    A) $1s^2 2s^2 2p^6 3s^2$
    B) $1s^2 2s^2 2p^2 3s^2$
    C) $1s^2 2s^6 2p^2 3s^2$
    D) $1s^2 2s^2 2p^2 3s^3$

3. List the following in order of decreasing electronegativity: fluorine (F), bromine (Br), magnesium (Mg), strontium (Sr).
    A) $F > Mg > Br > Sr$
    B) $F > Br > Mg > Sr$
    C) $Br > Mg > Sr > F$
    D) $Sr > Mg > Br > F$

Intramolecular Bonds

Chemical bonds, also called intramolecular bonds, are attractions between atoms that allow for the creation of substances consisting of more than one atom. When all the chemically bonded atoms are the same element, the substance is known as a **molecule**. When two or more different elements bond together, the result is called a **compound**. (However, the word *molecule* is often used colloquially to refer to both types of substances.)

Table 5.3. Common Molecules and Compounds	
H_2O	water
NaCl	table salt
CO_2	carbon dioxide
HCl	hydrochloric acid
O_3	ozone
$C_6H_{12}O_6$	glucose (sugar)
H_2	hydrogen gas

Types of Bonds

Not all chemical bonds are alike. Their causes vary, and thus the strength of those bonds also varies widely. There are two major types of bonds, distinguished from one another based on whether electrons are shared or transferred between the atoms. A **covalent bond** involves a pair of atoms sharing electrons from their outer orbitals to fill their valence shells. These bonds form between non-metals with similar electronegativities.

> **HELPFUL HINT**
>
> In a covalent bond, two atoms share electrons. In an ionic bond, one atom gives electrons to the other.

In an **ionic bond**, one atom "gives" its electrons to the other, resulting in one positively and one negatively charged atom. The bond is a result of the attraction between ions. Ionic bonds form between atoms with very different electronegativities.

Metals can form tightly packed arrays in which each atom is in close contact with many neighbors. So many atomic orbitals overlap with each atom that they form very large molecular orbitals that in turn overlap with each other creating a continuous band in which electrons can move. Any excitation, such as an electrical current, can cause the electrons to move throughout the array. The high electrical and thermal conductivity of metals is due to this ability of electrons to move throughout the lattice. This type of delocalized bonding is called **metallic bonding**. Metals are ductile or can be bent without breaking because the atoms can slide past each other without breaking the delocalized bonds.

Polarity

Polarity is the difference in charge across a compound caused by the uneven partial charge distribution between the atoms. Ionic bonds have higher polarity than covalent bonds because they consist of ions of full opposite charges, meaning one side of the compound is very positive and one very negative. The charge distribution in covalent bonds is more variable, resulting in either polar covalent bonds or non-polar covalent bonds.

Non-polar covalent bonds have no uneven distribution of charge. This is because electrons are completely shared between the two atoms, meaning neither has a strong hold on the shared electrons. Non-polar covalent bonds generally arise between two non-metal atoms with equal electronegativity, for example, two hydrogen atoms.

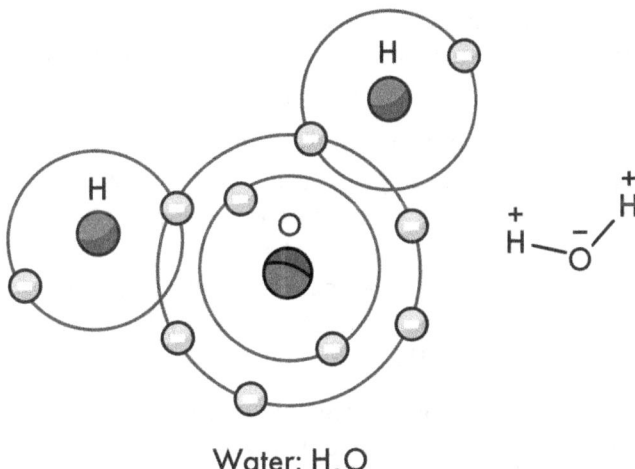

Water: H_2O

Polar covalent bonds arise between two non-metal atoms with different electronegativities. In these bonds, electrons are shared unequally. Neither atom is a completely charged ion; instead, the more electronegative atom will hold onto the electron more often, creating a slightly negative charge. The other atom will thus have a slightly positive charge. These slight charges are called **dipoles**.

A **dipole moment** is a measure of the unequal charge distribution in a polar bond. It is possible for a polar molecule to have no net dipole moment if the dipole moments of each bond are equal in magnitude and opposing in direction. These covalent compounds have a symmetrical molecular geometry, meaning that the dipoles created by the polar bond cancel each other out.

Practice Questions

4. Which of the following bonds would have the largest dipole moment?
    A) C – H
    B) C – F
    C) C – O
    D) C – N

5. Which group on the periodic table will typically adopt a charge of +1 when forming ionic compounds?
   A) alkaline earth metals
   B) lanthanides
   C) halogens
   D) alkali metals

Intermolecular Bonds

While intramolecular bonds occur within compounds to hold atoms together, it is also possible for bonds to exist between compounds. These intermolecular bonds do not result from the transfer or sharing of electrons. Rather, they are caused by the attraction between the positive and negative parts of separate compounds.

The force of attraction between hydrogen and an extremely electronegative atom, such as oxygen or nitrogen, is known as a **hydrogen bond**. For example, in water (H_2O), oxygen atoms are attracted to the hydrogen atoms in nearby molecules, creating hydrogen bonds. These bonds are significantly weaker than the chemical bonds that involve sharing or transfer of electrons, and have only 5 to 10 percent of the strength of a covalent bond. Despite its relative weakness, hydrogen bonding is quite important in the natural world; it has major effects on the properties of water and ice and is important biologically with regard to proteins and nucleic acids as well as the DNA double helix structure.

Van der Waals forces are electrical interactions between two or more molecules or atoms. They are the weakest type of intermolecular attraction, but if substantial amounts of these forces are present, their net effect can be quite strong.

There are two major types of van der Waals forces. The **London dispersion force** is a temporary force that occurs when electrons in two adjacent atoms form spontaneous, temporary dipoles due to the positions the atoms are occupying. This is the weakest intermolecular force and it does not exert a force over long distances. Interestingly, London dispersion forces are the only forces that exist between noble gas atoms; without these forces, noble gases would not be able to liquefy.

QUICK REVIEW

Why would molecules with large dipole moments be more likely to interact than non-polar molecules?

The second type of van der Waals force is **dipole-dipole interactions**, which are the result of two dipolar molecules interacting with each other. This interaction occurs when the partial positive dipole in one molecule is attracted to the partial negative dipole in the other molecule.

Practice Question

6. Which intermolecular forces would need to be considered in predicting the relative physical properties of CH_3F, CH_3Cl, CH_3Br, and CH_3I?
   A) London force only
   B) dipole-dipole and London force only
   C) dipole-dipole and hydrogen bonding only
   D) dipole-dipole, hydrogen bonding, and London force

Properties of Substances

Chemical and Physical Properties

Properties of substances are divided into two categories: physical and chemical. **Physical properties** are those which are measurable and can be seen without changing the chemical makeup of a substance. In contrast, **chemical properties** are those that determine how a substance will behave in a chemical reaction. These two categories differ in that a physical property may be identified just by observing, touching, or measuring the substance in some way; however, chemical properties cannot be identified simply by observing a material. Rather, the material must be engaged in a chemical reaction in order to identify its chemical properties.

> **HELPFUL HINT**
>
> In both physical and chemical changes, matter is always conserved, meaning it can never be created or destroyed.

Table 5.4. Physical and Chemical Properties

Physical Properties	Chemical Properties
temperature	heat of combustion
color	flammability
mass	toxicity
viscosity	chemical stability
density	enthalpy of formation

Mixtures

When substances are combined without a chemical reaction to bond them, the resulting substance is called a **mixture**. Physical changes can be used to separate mixtures. For example, heating salt water until the water evaporates, leaving the salt behind, will separate a salt water solution.

In a mixture, the components can be unevenly distributed, such as in trail mix or soil. These mixtures are described at **heterogeneous**. Alternatively, the components can be **homogeneously**, or uniformly, distributed, as in salt water.

A **solution** is a special type of stable homogenous mixture. The components of a solution will not separate on their own, and cannot be separated using a filter. The substance being dissolved is the **solute**, and the substance acting on the solute, or doing the dissolving, is the **solvent**.

Chemical Properties of Water

Though it is one of the most common and biologically essential compounds on Earth, water is chemically abnormal. Its chemical formula is H_2O, which means that water consists of one oxygen atom bound to two hydrogen atoms. The shape of this molecule is often described as looking like Mickey Mouse, with the oxygen atom in the middle as Mickey's face and the two hydrogen atoms as his ears.

Chemistry

This imbalanced shape means that oxygen has a slightly positive charge localized on the two hydrogen atoms, and a slightly negative charge on the lone oxygen. Because of this polarity, water molecules attract each other and tend to clump together, a property called **cohesion**. Water is also extremely **adhesive**, meaning it clings to other substances. These attractive forces account for a number of water's unique properties.

Water has a high **surface tension**, meaning the bonds between water molecules on the surface of a liquid are stronger than those beneath the surface. Surface tension makes it more difficult to puncture the surface of water. Combined with adhesion, it also helps cause **capillary action**, which is the ability of water to travel against gravity. Capillary action moves blood through vessels in the body and water from the roots to the leaves of plants.

Water is an efficient solvent for ionic compounds because of its hydrogen bonds and associated polarity. When ionic compounds like NaCl are placed in water, the individual ions are attracted to the opposite ends of the dipole moment in water. But water is stronger than the average solvent. In fact, it is known as the "universal solvent," because it is able to dissolve more substances than any other known liquid. The readiness with which ionic compounds dissolve in water is why so many minerals and nutrients are found naturally in water.

Water also has a low molecular weight. Most low-weight compounds exist in a gaseous form at room temperature, but water is a liquid at room temperature. Though water molecules have a relatively low weight, the boiling point and freezing point of water are abnormally high. This is because water's strong hydrogen bonds require high amounts of heat to break. These properties of water make it the only compound found naturally in all three phases—solid, liquid, and gas—on Earth.

Consistent with its high boiling point, water also has an unusually high specific heat index, meaning that water needs to absorb a lot of heat before it actually gets hot. This property allows the oceans to regulate global temperature, as they can absorb a large amount of energy.

Ice, or frozen water, is also abnormal. Normally molecules are tightly packed in the solid state, but water's hydrogen bonds form a crystalline lattice structure, placing molecules far apart. This extra space makes ice less dense than liquid water, which is why ice floats.

Osmosis, Diffusion, and Tonicity

Molecules and atoms have a tendency to spread out in space, moving from areas of high concentration to areas of lower concentration. This net movement is called **diffusion**. When solutions of differing concentrations are separated from each other by a porous membrane, the solvent molecules will flow across the membrane in order to equalize these different concentrations. This net movement of solvent particles is called **osmosis**. Osmosis is especially important in biological contexts, as cell and organelle membranes are semipermeable. Osmosis provides the main means by which water is transported in and out of cells.

> **HELPFUL HINT**
>
> An important characteristic of osmosis is that the solvent molecules are free to move across the membrane, but the solute cannot cross the membrane.

When two solutions are separated by a semipermeable membrane, their relative concentrations (which determine the direction of the movement of solute molecules) are called **tonicity**. This chemical property is typically used to describe the response of a cell when placed in a solvent.

Three types of tonicity are relevant in biological situations. **Hypertonic** solutions are those that have a higher concentration of a given solute than the interior of the cell. When placed in such solutions, the cell will lose solvent (water) as it travels to areas of higher solute concentration.

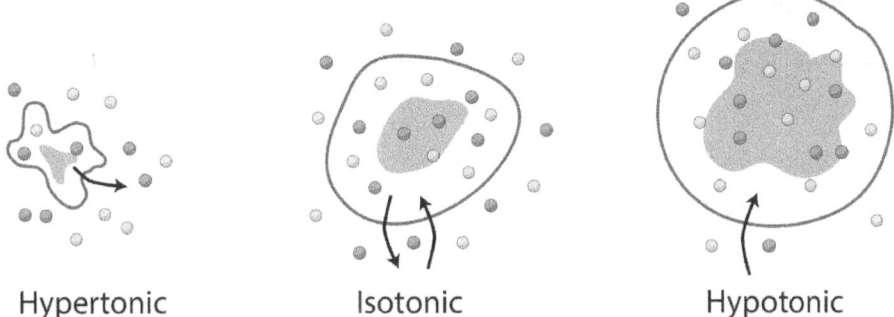

Hypertonic	Isotonic	Hypotonic

Hypotonicity refers to a solution that has a lower concentration of a given solute than the cell. Water will enter the cell, causing it to swell in response to hypotonic solutions.

Isotonic solutions are those in which solute concentration equals solute concentration inside the cell, and no net flux of solvent will occur between the cell and an isotonic solution.

Practice Questions

7. Which of the following is a chemical property?
    A) area
    B) boiling point
    C) solubility
    D) preferred oxidation state

8. The water glider is an insect that can walk on water. What property of water facilitates this ability?
    A) high surface tension
    B) osmosis
    C) tonicity
    D) ability of ice to float in water

States of Matter

All matter exists in one of four **states**: solid, liquid, gas, or plasma. **Solid** matter has densely packed molecules and does not change volume or shape. **Liquids** have more loosely packed molecules and can change shape but not volume. **Gas** molecules are widely dispersed, and gases can change both shape and volume. **Plasma** is similar to a gas but contains free-moving charged particles (although its overall charge is neutral).

Particles in gases, liquids, and solids all vibrate. Those in gases vibrate and move at high speeds; those in liquids vibrate and move slightly; those in solids vibrate yet stay packed in place in their rigid structure.

Changes in temperature and pressure can cause matter to change states. Generally, adding energy (in the form of heat) changes a substance to a higher energy state (e.g., solid to liquid). Transitions from a high to lower energy state (e.g., liquid to solid) release energy. Each of these changes has a specific name:

- solid to liquid: melting
- liquid to solid: freezing
- liquid to gas: evaporation
- gas to liquid: condensation
- solid to gas: sublimation
- gas to solid: deposition

The occurrence of these processes depends on the amount of energy in individual molecules, rather than the collective energy of the system. For example, in a pool of water outside on a hot day, the whole pool does not evaporate at once; evaporation occurs incrementally in molecules with a high enough energy. Evaporation is also more likely to occur in conjunction with a decrease in the gas pressure around a liquid, since molecules tend to move from areas of high pressure to areas of low pressure.

HELPFUL HINT

A *crystal* is a specific type of solid where atoms are arranged in a regular, repeating, geometric pattern known as a crystal lattice.

Phase diagrams are used to indicate the phase in which a substance is found at a given pressure and temperature. Phase diagrams are constructed on an *x, y*-coordinate system where temperature is plotted along the *x*-axis and pressure is plotted along the *y*-axis. Phase regions are areas on a phase diagram (corresponding to specific temperature and pressure combinations) at which the substance will exist in a particular physical phase. Lines called phase boundaries separate these phase regions, representing pressure and temperature combinations at which the substance undergoes phase transitions.

Every phase diagram includes two important points. The **triple point** is the point at which the lines of equilibrium intersect and all three phases (solid, liquid, and gas) exist in equilibrium. The second special point on a phase diagram is the **critical point**. This point is found along the phase boundary between liquid and gas, and is the point at which the phase boundary terminates. This represents the

Temperature fact that at very high temperature and pressure, liquid and gas phases become indistinguishable. This is known as a supercritical fluid.

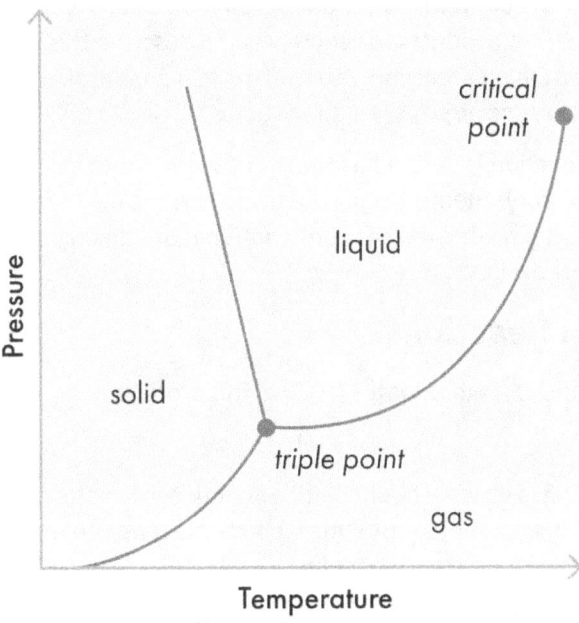

Practice Questions

9. Sublimation is the change from:
    A) gas to solid.
    B) liquid to solid.
    C) gas to liquid.
    D) solid to gas.

10. The process that takes place when water reaches its boiling point is called:
    A) condensation.
    B) evaporation.
    C) melting.
    D) sublimation.

Chemical Reactions

A **chemical reaction** involves some sort of chemical change in molecules, atoms, or ions when two or more of these interact. It is important to note that chemical reactions are not the same as state changes. For example, liquid water changing to ice is not a chemical reaction because water and ice have the same chemical properties, just different physical ones. A chemical reaction occurs between two reactants (substances) that form a new substance with different chemical properties than either of the two initial reactants.

Reactants are the substances that are consumed or altered in the chemical reaction, while **products** are substances formed as a result of the chemical reaction. Equations are usually written with the reactants on the left, the products on the right, and an arrow between them. The state of the chemical

compounds are sometimes noted using the labels *s* (solid), *l* (liquid), *g* (gas), or *aq* (aqueous, meaning a solution).

Chemical reactions generally occur in two directions. A reaction can move "forward" (from reactants to products), and in "reverse" (from products to reactants). To describe this, chemists say that the reaction occurs in two directions. Oftentimes, the arrow in a chemical equation has a head on each side, signifying that the reaction occurs in both directions.

The equilibrium point of a reaction is defined as the point where both the forward and reverse reactions are occurring at equal rates simultaneously—products are turning into reactants and reactants back into products. This produces a state in which, while the reaction is still taking place, no net change in concentration of reactants or products is occurring.

Balancing Chemical Reactions

In the equation below, H_2 and O_2, while water (H_2O) is the product.

$$2H_2 + O_2 \rightarrow 2H_2O$$

In this equation, the number 2 is called a coefficient, and it describes the number of atoms or molecules involved in the reaction. In this reaction, four hydrogen atoms (two molecules of H_2) react with two oxygen atoms. Note that the products also contain

four hydrogen and two oxygen molecules. When chemical equations are written, they must include the same number of each atom on both the reactant and product side of the arrow. This is an important step because chemical reactions adhere to the **law of conservation of matter**, which states that matter is neither created nor destroyed in a chemical reaction.

In order to balance the equation above, first examine the initial equation without coefficients, which looks like this:

$$H_2 + O_2 \rightarrow H_2O$$

This equation is unbalanced: there are two H atoms on each side, but the reactant side has two O atoms while the product side only has one. To fix this discrepancy, a coefficient of 2 is added in front of the product, H_2O, making the number of O atoms equal on both sides of the equation:

$$H_2 + O_2 \rightarrow 2H_2O$$

Now there are four H atoms on the product side while there are only 2 on the reactant side. This means that in order to finish balancing the equation, a coefficient of 2 must be added in front of H_2, so that there are four H atoms on the reactant side as well:

$$2H_2 + O_2 \rightarrow 2H_2O$$

Remember that in a chemical reaction, only the coefficients may be changed in order to balance it; the subscripts must not be changed. This would be like changing the actual chemical in the equation.

TYPES OF REACTIONS

There are several common types of chemical reactions, including decomposition, substitution, and combustion reactions.

Decomposition reactions are a common class of reaction, consisting of the separation of a compound into atoms or simpler molecules:

General Reaction: $AB \rightarrow A + B \quad 2H_2O_2 \rightarrow 2H_2O + O_2$

Single replacement reactions are those in which a part of one molecule is replaced by another atom or molecule. Reactivity in single substitutions is determined by the **activity series**: elements on the list will replace any element that is below it on the list (Table 5.5).

General Reaction: $AB + C \rightarrow AC + B \quad CH4 + Cl2 \rightarrow CH3Cl + HCl$

In a **double replacement** reaction, two parts of two different molecules swap places:

General Reaction: $AB + CD \rightarrow CB + AD \quad CuCl_2 + 2AgNO_3 \rightarrow Cu(NO_3)_2 + 2AgCl$

Table 5.5. Activity Series

Li	Ca	Mn	Ni	Cu
K	Na	Zn	Sn	Hg
Ba	Mg	Cr	Pb	Ag
Sr	Al	Fe	H₂	Pd
Pt	Au			

Combustion or burning reactions are high-temperature reactions in which a great deal of heat is released. In combustion reactions, oxygen is a reactant and carbon dioxide and water are produced. Because of the substantial amount of heat energy produced by combustion reactions, they have been important means of generating energy throughout human history, including combustion of fossil fuels, coal, and oil.

General Reaction:

$$CxHx + O_2 \rightarrow CO_2 + H_2O \quad 2C_8H_{18} + 25O_2 \rightarrow 16CO_2 + 18H_2O$$

Reaction Rates

are defined as those which produce energy, whereas **endothermic reactions** need energy in order to occur. Regardless of whether energy is absorbed or released overall, every chemical reaction requires a certain amount of energy in order to begin. This amount is referred to as the **activation energy**.

Collisions of reactant particles supply the activation energy for a reaction. The more particles collide, the more energy will be produced. Thus, the more often particles collide, the more likely a reaction is to occur. However, it is quite possible that though some particles collide, not enough energy is generated for an actual reaction to occur.

Given the variability in activation energies of a reaction, as well as variation in the frequency of reactant particle collisions, not all chemical reactions occur at the same rate. A number of variables affect the rate of reaction, including temperature, pressure, concentration, and surface area. The higher the temperature, pressure and concentration, the more likely particles are to collide and thus the reaction rate will be higher. The same is true of surface area for a reaction between a solid and a liquid in which it is immersed. The larger the surface area, the more solid reactant particles are in contact with liquid particles, and the faster the reaction occurs.

Practice Questions

11. When following chemical equation for the combustion of methanol (CH_3OH) is balanced, what is the coefficient of H_2O?

$$\_CH_3OH + O_2 \to CO_2 + H_2O$$

A) 3
B) 2
C) 1
D) 4

12. hos is the following reaction classified?

$$2KCLO_3 \to 2KCL + 3O_2$$

A) decomposition
B) combustion
C) substitution
D) double displacement

13. What is the missing product in the following combustion reaction?

$$C_{10}H_8 + 12O_2 \to H\_2O + \to$$

A) CO
B) CH_4
C) CO_2
D) $C_2H_3O_2$

Catalysts

Catalysts reduce the amount of energy that a chemical reaction needs in order to happen, so that the reaction can occur more easily. However, the catalyst itself remains chemically unchanged and is not consumed at all in the reaction. A catalyst lowers the **activation energy** needed for a reaction to take place, and it will change the rate of both directions of the reaction.

Catalysts function by one of two main methods. The first is **adsorption**, where particles stick to the surface of the catalyst and move around, increasing their likelihood of collision. A more complicated method is the creation of **intermediate compounds** which are unstable and then break down into other substances, leaving the catalyst in its original state. Many enzymes (proteins which function as catalysts), which are discussed below, work via the creation of intermediate compounds.

If the rate of a chemical reaction can be increased, it can also be decreased. **Inhibitors** are essentially the opposite of catalysts, and they act to slow down the reaction rate or even stop the reaction altogether. Inhibitors are used for various reasons, including giving scientists more control over reactions. Both inhibitors and catalysts naturally play significant roles in the chemical reactions that occur in human bodies.

Enzymes

Enzymes are efficient catalysts functioning in biochemical reactions. They are large, soluble protein molecules that serve to speed up chemical reactions in cells. Cellular respiration, DNA replication, digestion, protein synthesis, and photosynthesis are common processes, all essential for life, that are catalyzed with enzymes.

> **HELPFUL HINT**
>
> Enzyme inhibitors will typically function by binding to an enzyme and thereby preventing it from functioning.

Like other types of catalysts, enzymes take part in a reaction to provide an alternative pathway with a smaller activation energy, but they remain unchanged themselves. However, enzymes only alter the reaction rate; they do not actually change the equilibrium point of a reaction. Also, unlike most chemical catalysts, enzymes are very selective, which means that they only catalyze certain reactions. (Many other types of catalysts catalyze a variety of reactions.)

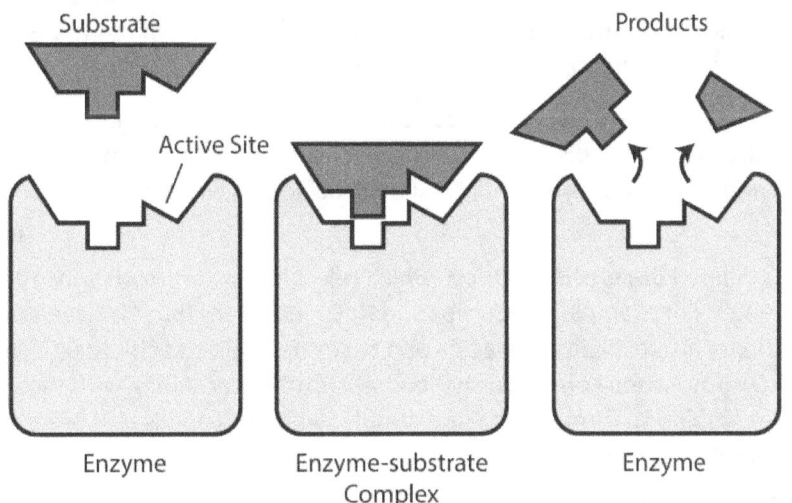

> **HELPFUL HINT**
>
> As suggested by the lock and key model, enzymes are typically highly specific to the reaction they catalyze. In a cellular context, why would it be detrimental if enzymes universally catalyzed any reaction?

This particular aspect of enzyme behavior is referred to as the **lock and key model**. This alludes to the fact that not all keys can open all locks; most keys can only open specific locks. Similarly, the shape of any one enzyme only matches the shape of the molecule it reacts with, called a **substrate**. The **active site** is the place on the enzyme that directly contacts the substrate, or the place where the two "puzzle pieces" fit together facilitating the actual reaction.

Enzymes have a characteristic optimum temperature at which they function best and require a sufficient substrate concentration. The reason for these restrictions is that variables like temperature and pH affect the shape of an enzyme's active site. In fact, if the temperature is increased too much, usually past 60 degrees Celsius, an enzyme can become **denatured**. This means that the active site has undergone a permanent change in shape, so it can no longer serve its purpose as a catalyst.

> **Practice Question**
>
> 14. A catalyst increases a reaction rate by
> A)   increasing the activation energy.
> B)   increasing the concentration of the reactants
> C)   changing the relative partial pressures of the reactants
> D)   changing the reaction mechanism

Acids and Bases

Many scientists have attempted to define and differentiate the properties of acids and bases throughout the centuries. As far back as the sixteenth century, Robert Boyle noted that acids are corrosive, sour, and change the color of vegetable dyes like litmus from blue to red. On the other hand, bases, or alkaline solutions are slippery, bitter, and change the color of litmus from red to blue. The litmus test is still used today to determine whether a solution is acidic or basic.

Later, Svante Arrhenius gave an even more specific definition of acids and bases. He defined **acids** as compounds that ionize when they dissolve in water, releasing H+ ions along with a negative ion called a **counterion**. For example, the well-known acid HCl (hydrochloric acid) dissolves into H+ and Cl- ions in water.

Similarly, Arrhenius defined bases as substances which release OH- ions (hydroxide) and a positive ion when dissolved in water. For example, the compound NaOH dissolves into Na+ (the counterion) and OH- ions in water. His theory also explains why acids and bases neutralize each other. If acids have an H+ ion and bases have an OH- ion, when combined the ions will form water. Along with the water, the counterions usually combine to form a salt. For example, when HCl and NaOH are combined, the result is water and table salt (H_2O and NaCl).

Thomas Lowry and J.N. Bronsted later presented a revised theory of acids and bases. In the Bronsted-Lowry definition of acids and bases, acids are defined as proton donors and bases as proton acceptors. An acid and base are always paired as reactants. The base reactant produces a **conjugate acid** as a product, paired with a **conjugate base** produced from the reactant acid. Water, often involved in these reactions, can either accept or donate a proton, meaning that it can act as either an acid or a base, depending on the particular equation.

In the example below, acetic acid (CH_3CO_2H) is dissolved in water, producing a conjugate base (CH_3CO^-). Water acts as the base, and its conjugate acid is the hydronium ion (H_3O+).

$$\underset{\text{acid}}{CH_3CO_2H} + \underset{\text{base}}{H_2O} \rightarrow \underset{\text{conjugate base}}{CH_3CO_2^-} + \underset{\text{conjugate acid}}{H_3O^+}$$

This is perhaps easiest to understand when considering the definition of hydrogen cations. H+ is essentially a lone proton, and may act as an acid, being donated to another molecule. If it is in a solution of water, it can combine with water to form hydronium, H_3O+, which is always an acid as it is a proton acceptor.

The strength of an acid or base is measured on the pH scale, which ranges from 1 – 14, with 1 being the strongest acid, 14 the strongest base, and 7

> **HELPFUL HINT**
>
> Any base containing a Group 1 or Group 2 metal is a strong base.

being neutral. A substance's pH value is a measure of how many hydrogen ions are in the solution. The scale is exponential, meaning an acid with a pH of 3 has ten times as many hydrogen ions as an acid with a pH of 4. Water, which separates into equal numbers of hydrogen and hydroxide ions, has a neutral pH of 7.

Strong acids and bases are defined as those that completely ionize in water. Other acids and bases are considered weak, which means that they only partially ionize in water.

Table 5.6. Strong Acids and Bases	
Strong Acids	**Strong Bases**
HI	NaOH
HBr	KOH
$HClO_4$	LiOH
$HClO_3$	RbOH
HCl	CsOH
HNO_3	$Ca(OH)_2$
H_2SO_4	$Ba(OH)_2$
HIO_4	$Sr(OH)_2$

Practice Questions

15. Which is NOT a definition of an acid?
    A) A substance that contains hydrogen and produces H+ in water.
    B) A substance that donates protons to a base.
    C) A substance that reacts with a base to form a salt and water.
    D) A substance that accepts protons.

16. Which of the following is NOT a strong acid?
    A) $HCLO_3$
    B) $HCLO_4$
    C) HNO_3
    D) HNO_2

Answer Key

1. D: Atomic radius increases from the top of the periodic table to the bottom and also from right to left. This means that the largest atoms are found in the lower left-hand corner of the periodic table while the smallest are found in the upper right-hand corner. Of the three elements listed, xenon has the smallest radius, barium is larger as it is further down and to the left, and cesium is the largest as it is furthest to the left of the three: Xe < Ba < Cs.

2. A: Mg has an atomic number of 12 on the periodic table, meaning it has 12 protons and 12 electrons. These 12 electrons are assigned to orbitals in the order:

$$1s^2 2s^2 2p^6 3s^2$$

3. B: Electronegativity generally increases from bottom to top and from right to left on the periodic table. This means that the most electronegative atoms are at the top right of the table. Thus, of the elements listed, F is the most electronegative, followed by Br, Mg, and then Sr with the lowest electronegativity: F > Br > Mg > Sr.

4. B: The difference in electronegativity is the greatest between carbon and fluorine, so the C—F bond will have the largest dipole moment.

5. D: The alkali metals have a full valence shell when they lose one electron, so they easily form ions of +1.

6. B: These molecules are polar and so are subject to both dipole-dipole and London forces. There are no hydrogen atoms bound to high electronegative atoms, so there will be no hydrogen bonding.

7. D: Area, boiling point, and solubility are all physical properties that can be measured without undergoing a chemical reaction. The preferred oxidation state of a metal cannot be identified in any way except through a chemical reaction, and is thus a chemical property.

8. A: The high surface tension of water, which is a byproduct of hydrogen bonding, allows the water glider to walk on water.

9. D: Sublimation is when matter changes from a solid to a gas.

10. B: Evaporation is the process of conversion from liquid to gas that occurs at the boiling point.

11. D: The same number of C and O atoms appear on both sides, so start by balancing for H:

$$\_\_CH_3OH + \_\_O_2 \rightarrow CO_2 + 2H_2O$$

Next, add a coefficient on the left to balance O:

$$2CH_3OH + \_\_O_2 \rightarrow \_\_CO_2 + 2H_2O$$

Next, add or change coefficients to balance C and H:

$$2CH_3OH + \_\_O_2 \rightarrow 2CO_2 + 4H_2O$$

Finally, add coefficients to balance O:

$$2CH_3OH + 3O_2 \rightarrow 2CO_2 + 4H_2O$$

12. A: This reaction has a single reactant compound and produces simpler molecules. It is therefore a decomposition reaction.

13. C: All combustion reactions produce H_2O and CO_2, so the missing product is CO_2.

14. D: A catalyst reduces the activation energy by creating an alternative reaction mechanism for the reaction.

15. D: Acids increase the concentration of hydrogen ions in solution and do not accept protons.

16. D: HNO_2 is not a strong acid. All the other choices are strong acids.

Practice Test

Verbal Skills

Directions: Read the question, and then choose the most correct answer.

1. Omari felt *apathetic* in his employment, so he decided to quit his job and go to nursing school. *Apathetic* means
    A) motivated.
    B) furious.
    C) indifferent.
    D) unsure.

2. Hank was drunk and *belligerent* because his wife left him. *Belligerent* means
    A) hostile.
    B) sad.
    C) angry.
    D) loud.

3. After years of daily observing people in the worst situations of their lives, Austin's behavior became *callous*. *Callous* means
    A) mean.
    B) insensitive.
    C) annoyed.
    D) empathetic.

4. Cheryl was nervous, but she did not want to *hinder* her daughter's dream of becoming a paramedic. *Hinder* means
    A) encourage.
    B) expedite.
    C) crush.
    D) impede.

5. Clyde was *lucid* when he told the paramedics who shot him. *Lucid* means
    A) confused.
    B) rational.
    C) emotional.
    D) incomprehensible.

6. Larry thought his neighbor, John, was *pilfering* Larry's morning newspaper, so he reported him to the constable. *Pilfering* means
   A) stealing.
   B) borrowing.
   C) moving.
   D) returning.

7. Blanca had an *inconspicuous* scar on her arm from a car accident several years earlier. *Inconspicuous* means
   A) large.
   B) prominent.
   C) unnoticeable.
   D) small.

8. Julian became *frantic* when he realized his child was missing. *Frantic* means
   A) frenzied.
   B) calm.
   C) frustrated.
   D) alert.

9. Henry only *exacerbated* the problem when he poured water on a grease fire. *Exacerbated* means
   A) hurt.
   B) reduced.
   C) aggravated.
   D) excited.

10. The hospital administrator writes reports that tend to be *verbose*. *Verbose* means
    A) concise.
    B) clear.
    C) confusing.
    D) wordy.

11. One purpose of nursing is to *foster* positive relationships between health care practitioners and patients. *Foster* means
    A) alleviate.
    B) create.
    C) discourage.
    D) promote.

12. It is impossible to *quantify* the damage resulting from the pandemic. *Quantify* means
    A) measure.
    B) understand.
    C) extend.
    D) improve.

Use the following passage for questions 13–18.

Most people think of respiration as the mechanical exchange of air between human lungs and the environment. They think about oxygen filling up the tiny air sacs in the lungs. They think about how this process feeds the capillaries surrounding the air sacs, which then infuse the bloodstream with the oxygen it needs. They may even think about how carbon dioxide is exhaled from the lungs back into the environment. But this process—known as external respiration—is just one form of respiration that occurs in the human body. Did you know there are actually two types of respiration in humans? The second form of respiration is equally important; it is known as internal, or cellular, respiration.

Whereas external respiration centers on an exchange between the lungs and the environment, internal respiration centers on a molecular exchange between cells and capillaries. All organs inside the human body rely on cellular respiration to function properly. Cells within the organs are surrounded by thousands of tiny capillaries that act as channels for the exchange of gases. Oxygen is carried through these microscopic blood vessels, moving from red blood cells to the surrounding tissue. Additionally, built-up carbon dioxide in the tissues flows through the capillaries back to the lungs. This second form of respiration may be invisible to the human eye, but it is crucial for the maintenance of human life.

13. Which of the following statements can the reader infer from the passage?
    A) The author believes that most people know what capillaries are.
    B) The idea that the human lungs contain tiny air sacs is a myth.
    C) The term "external respiration" does not accurately describe breathing.
    D) The author believes that most people have never heard of internal respiration.

14. Which sentence best summarizes the passage's main idea?
    A) "Most people think of respiration as the mechanical exchange of air between human lungs and the environment."
    B) "They may even think about how carbon dioxide is exhaled from the lungs back into the environment."
    C) "The second form of respiration is equally important; it is known as internal, or cellular, respiration."
    D) "Cells within the organs are surrounded by thousands of tiny capillaries that act as channels for the exchange of gases."

15. According to the passage, external respiration is an exchange between what and what?
    A) the lungs and the environment
    B) oxygen and carbon dioxide
    C) capillaries and cells
    D) blood vessels and blood cells

16. What is the author's primary purpose in writing this essay?
    A) to inform readers about external and internal respiration
    B) to advise readers about ways to treat patients with lung disease
    C) to prove that most people are ignorant about internal respiration
    D) to persuade readers to take better care of their lungs and other organs

17. According to the passage, how does carbon dioxide escape during internal respiration?
    A) The lungs draw it into tiny air sacs.
    B) The lungs release it into the bloodstream.
    C) It travels from the tissues through the capillaries back to the lungs.
    D) It travels from the capillaries into the red blood cells to the tissues.

18. How does the author define the word *capillaries* in the passage?
    A) "tiny air sacs" (paragraph 1)
    B) "two types of respiration" (paragraph 1)
    C) "all organs inside the human body" (paragraph 2)
    D) "these microscopic blood vessels" (paragraph 2)

Use the following passage for questions 19–24.

In 1733, Stephen Hales, an English clergyman with a great interest in a variety of sciences, experimented with inserting tubes into the arteries of animals such as horses to measure "the force of the blood," thereby becoming the first person to measure blood pressure. He described his findings in a study titled *Haemastaticks*, noting how high the blood would rise in the tube's column as he entered it into the animals' arteries.

Fortunately, we no longer have to use such invasive methods to study blood pressure. In 1896, Italian physician Scipione Riva-Rocci, building on earlier noninvasive methods of measuring blood pressure, created what we still recognize as a sphygmomanometer, the conventional blood pressure meter that we use today.

Shortly after Riva-Rocci's invention was made available to the medical world, Nikolai Korotkov, a Russian surgeon, combined the use of a sphygmomanometer with a stethoscope to create a new way to monitor blood pressure, the auscultatory (listening) technique. The cuff of the sphygmomanometer is placed around the patient's upper arm and tightened enough to stop the blood flow. It is then released gradually while a health care provider listens with the stethoscope and monitors a column of liquid mercury on the sphygmomanometer. Even though we now also have digital methods that do not use mercury, blood pressure is still described in millimeters of mercury (mm Hg). Discoveries and inventions from more than one hundred years ago still form the basis of the way we measure blood pressure today.

19. Which sentence best summarizes the passage?
    A) "In 1733, Stephen Hales, an English clergyman with a great interest in a variety of sciences, experimented with inserting tubes into the arteries of animals such as horses to measure 'the force of the blood,' thereby becoming the first person to measure blood pressure."
    B) "In 1896, Italian physician Scipione Riva-Rocci, building on earlier noninvasive methods of measuring blood pressure, created what we still recognize as a sphygmomanometer, the conventional blood pressure meter that we use today."
    C) "The cuff of the sphygmomanometer is placed around the patient's upper arm and tightened enough to stop the blood flow."
    D) "Discoveries and inventions from more than one hundred years ago still form the basis of the way we measure blood pressure today."

20. What is the author's primary purpose in writing this essay?
    A) to provide biographies of Hales, Riva-Rocci, and Korotkov
    B) to provide a history of inventions that measure blood pressure
    C) to explain how medical professionals measure blood pressure today
    D) to warn readers to avoid contact with mercury, which is poisonous

21. Which of the following statements can be considered a statement of FACT according to the content offered in the paragraphs above?
    A) Doctor Hales was a veterinarian who measured farm animals' blood pressure in the 1700s.
    B) Doctor Korotkov invented the stethoscope, a new way to "listen" to patients' blood pressure.
    C) Doctor Riva-Rocci invented the earliest version of the sphygmomanometer, a blood pressure meter.
    D) Today, a health care provider listens with a stethoscope and monitors a column of liquid mercury on the sphygmomanometer.

22. The author begins paragraph 2 with the word *fortunately* because he or she thinks we are lucky to have
    A) excellent health care that is not very expensive.
    B) ways to treat hypertension and low blood pressure.
    C) noninvasive methods of measuring blood pressure.
    D) animals that doctors can use in invasive experiments.

23. According to the passage, what is true of mercury?
    A) Using a sphygmomanometer, we still use mercury to measure blood pressure.
    B) We still describe blood pressure in millimeters of mercury (mm Hg).
    C) Using a stethoscope, we still use mercury to "listen" to blood pressure.
    D) In invasive treatments, we still insert tubes of mercury into horses' arteries.

24. Like a shirt cuff, a blood-pressure cuff
    A) buttons at the wrist.
    B) encircles part of the arm.
    C) is made of heavy cloth.
    D) cuts off the blood flow.

Use the following passage for questions 25–30.

Water accounts for roughly 60 percent of an adult human's body weight and is essential for most bodily functions. Dehydration is a deficit of water in the body. It can be caused by illness, exercise, heat, stress, or lack of self-care, and its effects range from a simple headache to cardiac arrest.

Throughout the day, humans continuously lose water through urine, feces, breath, and skin. If you are waiting until you are thirsty to drink something, then you are already dehydrated; our thirst mechanism fails to "notify" our body of dehydration in time. Mild dehydration is easily remedied, but dehydration can affect brain capacity, motor skills, and attention. Severe or chronic cases of dehydration have more dramatic effects. It can damage your kidneys, increase your heart rate to the point of cardiac arrest, cause you to collapse or faint, or force your body into a state of hyperthermia.

Under normal circumstances, all of this can be prevented by replenishing fluids throughout the day. The amount of water an individual needs varies based on such factors as metabolism or diet, but <u>conventional wisdom</u> is that humans should take in anywhere between 2.7 and 3.7 liters of water each day. This intake can come from various sources, including juices and foods with high water content, such as fruits and vegetables.

25. Which of the following statements can the reader infer from the passage?
    A) Most headaches are a result of dehydration.
    B) The human body does not "notify" us when it is dehydrated.
    C) Dehydration is a medical problem, but it is not life threatening.
    D) Doctors say we should drink eight full glasses of water each day.

26. In the third paragraph, what does the phrase *conventional wisdom* mean?
    A) conservative thinking
    B) unadventurous precautions
    C) standard guidelines
    D) casual suggestions

27. What is the author's primary purpose in writing this essay?
    A) to advise readers on ways to treat patients with severe dehydration
    B) to warn readers that dehydration can kill patients
    C) to explain what dehydration is and how it can be prevented
    D) to tell a story about someone who was successfully treated for dehydration

28. In the first sentence, what does the word *essential* mean?
    A) basic
    B) helpful
    C) crucial
    D) preferred

29. Which sentence best summarizes the passage's main idea?
    A) An adult human's body is 60 percent water.
    B) Severe dehydration can cause kidney damage, cardiac arrest, fainting, or hyperthermia.
    C) Every person needs to drink between 2.7 and 3.7 liters of water each day.
    D) Dehydration has a variety of causes and a range of effects, from mild to severe.

30. According to the passage, what causes dehydration?
    A) illness, exercise, heat, stress, or lack of self-care
    B) urine, feces, breath, and skin
    C) kidney damage, cardiac arrest, fainting, or hyperthermia
    D) juices, fruits, and vegetables

Use the following passage for questions 31–36.

E-cigarettes have only been around for about fifteen years, but they are a booming business. E-cigarettes do not contain tobacco; instead, they contain a liquid that is heated to produce an aerosol that is then inhaled. The liquid usually contains nicotine, the primary addictive substance in tobacco. Some political officials and health professionals are likening e-cigarettes—in spite of their modern electronic disguise—to their tobacco-laden predecessors, questioning the health effects of inhaling some of the liquid's other ingredients. Consequently, debates over e-cigarettes are currently being waged in schools, households, legislatures, and science labs across the globe.

Politicians and health experts are pressing governments to regulate e-cigarettes because they believe their popularity will undermine public health gains made in the decades-long war on traditional smoking. Other medical professionals believe e-cigarettes may, in fact, help this war by providing smokers with an alternative to smoking tobacco, which, in addition to nicotine, contains many harmful substances and is unequivocally linked with multiple types of cancer.

Scientists have been researching the health effects of e-cigarettes. Recent studies, unfortunately, have created more questions than answers. While one trial showed that e-cigarettes may be as effective as nicotine patches in helping people quit smoking, another showed that e-cigarette vapor may contain metal that could cause "popcorn lung." As we await answers, the growth of the e-cigarette industry looks like it is not going to slow in the near future: e-cigarettes manufacturing and sales is a multibillion-dollar industry that is likely going to continue stirring debate in the decades to come.

31. Which of the following is NOT listed as a detail in the passage?
    A) Instead of tobacco, e-cigarettes contain a liquid; the liquid is heated to produce an aerosol that the e-cigarette user inhales.
    B) Like cigarettes made from tobacco, e-cigarettes contain nicotine, which is addictive.
    C) Like cigarettes made from tobacco, e-cigarettes cause lung cancer, studies have shown.
    D) One study showed that e-cigarettes can help people quit smoking cigarettes containing tobacco.

32. What is the author's primary purpose in writing this essay?
    A) to reassure readers that it is safe to smoke e-cigarettes
    B) to inform readers that scientists do not yet know all the effects of e-cigarette smoking
    C) to warn readers about cause-effect relationships between e-cigarette smoking and cancer
    D) to persuade readers to quit smoking tobacco and start "vaping" e-cigarettes

33. What is the meaning of the word *booming* in the first paragraph?
    A) loud
    B) bellowing
    C) successful
    D) selling

34. Readers can infer from reading this passage that smoking e-cigarettes
    A) probably causes cancer.
    B) is no less harmful than smoking tobacco.
    C) is usually addictive.
    D) is as pleasurable as smoking tobacco.

35. Which of the following statements can the reader infer from the passage?
    A) The author thinks it is very wrong to make and sell e-cigarettes.
    B) The author believes quitting tobacco smoking is a positive step.
    C) In the author's opinion, e-cigarettes are just as harmful as cigarettes made with tobacco.
    D) The author has no opinions about any of the content in the passage.

36. Which sentence best summarizes the passage's main idea?
    A) "E-cigarettes do not contain tobacco; instead, they contain a liquid that is heated to produce an aerosol that is then inhaled."
    B) "Some political officials and health professionals are likening e-cigarettes— in spite of their modern electronic disguise—to their tobacco-laden predecessors, questioning the health effects of inhaling some of the liquid's other ingredients."
    C) "Other medical professionals believe e-cigarettes may, in fact, help this war by providing smokers with an alternative to smoking tobacco, which, in addition to nicotine, contains many harmful substances and is unequivocally linked with multiple types of cancer."
    D) "As we await answers, the growth of the e-cigarette industry looks like it is not going to slow in the near future: e-cigarettes manufacturing and sales is a multibillion-dollar industry that is likely going to continue stirring debate in the decades to come."

Use the following passage for questions 37–42.

New studies indicate that the impact of a single concussion, even if it is a person's first, can cause longer-lasting neurological damage than we previously knew—possibly even permanent. This changes the ways school districts and medical professionals are treating high school students who experience concussions. Many high school athletes return to their respective sports just one or two weeks after sustaining a concussion, but research shows that clinical symptoms of a concussion can continue for up to six months after the initial injury.

Even more troubling is the evidence that damage caused by a concussion may be permanent. The brain is commonly known for its fragility; ironically, it may be its resiliency that is hiding the long-term effects of concussions. A concussion is a mild traumatic brain injury. The brain is tremendously resilient in how it deals with the damage: it can "rewire" around the area of trauma and make new neurological connections. The consequence of this "rewiring" is that we may not recognize the extent of a brain injury. If students return to play too soon, they can exacerbate the initial damage or prolong the side effects.

37. Which sentence best summarizes the passage's main idea?
    A) Due to new studies, school districts are now requiring injured athletes to wait for six months before returning to play.
    B) Following a concussion, it is probably advisable for a student athlete to wait up to six months before returning to play.
    C) The human brain is so resilient that it can heal from a concussion by "rewiring" around the traumatized area.
    D) The human brain is too fragile to heal from even a mild concussion within two weeks.

38. What is the meaning of the word *resiliency* in the second paragraph?
    A) deceitfulness
    B) ability to heal quickly
    C) ability to quietly endure
    D) mild sarcasm

39. Which of the following is NOT listed as a detail in the passage?
    A) New studies show that permanent brain damage can possibly result from a concussion.
    B) In the past, school coaches have insisted that injured athletes resume playing too soon.
    C) After sustaining concussions, many high school athletes begin playing again after two weeks.
    D) The brain can "rewire" around an injured area and make new neurological connections.

40. What is the author's primary purpose in writing this essay?
    A) to reassure readers that teenagers' brains can quickly heal following concussions
    B) to suggest that, following a concussion, a student athlete should take several months off to heal
    C) to scare readers about cause-effect relationships between sports injuries and permanent brain damage
    D) to persuade readers not to allow their children to play high-school sports such as football

41. Readers can infer from reading this passage that concussions are
    A) more harmful than researchers knew in the past.
    B) less harmful than researchers thought in the past.
    C) not serious due to the brain's remarkable resiliency.
    D) uncommon among high school and college athletes.

42. In the first sentence, what does the word *neurological* mean?
    A) physical
    B) psychological
    C) having to do with the brain
    D) having to do with athletic injuries

Use the following passage for questions 43–48.

Have you ever wondered why exactly we feel pain when we get hurt? Or why some patients feel phantom pain even in the absence of a real trauma or damage? Pain is a highly sophisticated biological mechanism, one that is often down-played or misinterpreted. Pain is much more than a measure of tissue damage—it is a complex neurological chain reaction that sends sensory data to the brain. Pain is not produced by the toe you stubbed; rather, it is produced once the information about the "painful" incident reaches the brain. The brain analyzes the sensory signals emanating from the toe you stubbed, but the toe itself is not producing the sensation of pain.

In most cases, the brain offers accurate interpretations of the sensory data that is sent to it via the neurological processes in the body. If you hold your hand too close to a fire, for instance, the brain triggers pain that causes you to jerk your hand away, preventing further damage.

Phantom pain, most commonly associated with the amputation or loss of a limb, on the other hand, is triggered even in the absence of any injury. One possible explanation is that the spinal cord is still processing sensations from that area.

The science of pain management is complex and still poorly understood. However, anesthetics or anti-inflammatory medications can reduce or relieve pain by disrupting the neurological pathways that produce it. The absence of pain, however, is a double-edged sword—sometimes pain is the only clue to an underlying injury or disease. Likewise, an injury or disease can dull or eliminate pain, making it impossible to sense when something is actually wrong.

43. Readers can infer from the passage that pain is
    A) simple: pain is painful.
    B) more complicated than most people know.
    C) caused by the body's system of endocrine glands.
    D) often exaggerated in patients' minds.

44. What does the term *phantom pain* mean in the first and third paragraphs?
    A) ghostly pain
    B) pain that is *not* the result of an injury
    C) mild pain
    D) pain that is "a double-edged sword"

45. Which sentence best summarizes the passage's main idea?
    A) Pain is a complicated biological process, one that many people misjudge or do not understand.
    B) Many people wonder why we feel pain when we are injured, or why some patients feel phantom pain.
    C) When you stub your toe, your brain analyzes the sensory signals coming from your injury.
    D) Anti-inflammatory medications can lessen or ease pain by affecting neurological processes.

46. According to the passage, what is true of phantom pain?
    A) It is psychological, not physical; in other words, it is not real.
    B) Biologists are mystified by this kind of pain.
    C) It occurs because the body remembers how painful it felt when a limb was severely injured.
    D) It may happen because the spinal cord is still processing sensations from an amputated limb.

47. On which system of the human body does the author focus in this passage?
    A) the neurological system
    B) the immune system
    C) the circulatory system
    D) the cardiovascular system

48. In the last paragraph, the phrase "a double-edged sword" means that the absence of pain can be
    A) positive or negative.
    B) mild or unbearable.
    C) caused by knife wounds.
    D) even more painful than pain.

Use the following passage for questions 49–54.

Many snakes produce a toxic fluid in their salivary glands called venom. The two key ingredients in all snake venoms are enzymes and polypeptides. Some enzymes help the snake disable its prey, and others help the snake digest its prey. The victim of the snakebite has a much less beneficial experience with these enzymes: snake venoms can speed up chemical reactions that lower blood pressure, paralyze muscles, destroy tissues, deconstruct red blood cells, or cause internal bleeding.

There are many different types of snake venom, composed of various combinations of toxic and nontoxic substances. Toxins in snake venom are often divided into three categories: hemotoxins, neurotoxins, and cytotoxins. Hemotoxins affect the blood by interfering with the process of blood coagulation. In some cases, hemotoxins inhibit the process of blood clotting, and in other cases they cause excessive clotting. Neurotoxins target the nervous system rather than body tissues; they disrupt the messages sent by neurotransmitter production and reception throughout the body. Neurotoxins can paralyze muscles, causing respiratory failure and possibly death. Cytotoxins cause liquefactive necrosis of body cells; they dissolve cells, leading to the death of tissues or organs. Some cytotoxins target specific types of cells—myotoxins affect muscles, cardiotoxins attack the heart, and nephrotoxins damage the kidneys.

In addition to research on various antivenoms to combat the potentially deadly effects of snake venom, scientists have also been looking at the venom itself as a possible source of medical benefits. Researchers have been studying the chemical compositions of these venoms and have been making strides in using the science behind the toxins to combat major diseases such as cancer, heart disease, and Alzheimer's. For instance, a drug called captopril, used to treat hypertension, is based on a toxin in the venom of a pit viper found in Brazil.

49. Which sentence best summarizes the passage's main idea?
    A) "Many snakes produce a toxic fluid in their salivary glands called venom."
    B) "There are many different types of snake venom, composed of various combinations of toxic and nontoxic substances."
    C) "Some cytotoxins target specific types of cells—myotoxins affect muscles, cardiotoxins attack the heart, and nephrotoxins damage the kidneys."
    D) "Researchers have been studying the chemical compositions of these venoms and have been making strides in using the science behind the toxins to combat major diseases such as cancer, heart disease, and Alzheimer's."

50. In the last paragraph, what does the word *strides* mean?
    A) long steps
    B) heavy stomping
    C) improvements
    D) experiments

51. In the last sentence in the second paragraph, what does the word part *nephro* in the word *nephrotoxins* probably mean?
    A) poison
    B) heart
    C) muscle
    D) kidney

52. According to the passage, how does venom benefit snakes, besides the fact that this fluid allows snakes to kill their prey?
    A) It helps snakes to disable and digest their prey.
    B) It can heal snakes' diseases such as cancer and Alzheimer's.
    C) It terrifies snakes' prey, momentarily paralyzing these creatures.
    D) It discourages other predators from pursuing and eating snakes.

53. What is the author's primary purpose in writing this essay?
    A) to advise readers on ways to treat patients with snakebites
    B) to warn readers that most snakes are venomous
    C) to inform readers about the contents of snake venom
    D) to tell a story about a scientist who used venom as a medicine

54. Which of the following statements can the reader infer from the passage?
    A) All snakes produce venom.
    B) Some snakes are not venomous.
    C) A venomous snake never bites other members of its own species.
    D) A Brazilian pit viper's venom is not poisonous to humans.

Use the following passage for questions 55–60.

The discovery of penicillin by Alexander Fleming in 1928 revolutionized medical care. The widespread use of penicillin and other antibiotics has saved millions of people from the deadliest bacterial infections known to humans and prevented the spread of bacterial diseases. But we have relied on antibiotics too heavily, which has undermined their effectiveness as bacteria evolve resistance to these drugs.

To add to the problem, factory farms across the United States are inundating pigs, cattle, chickens, and turkeys with cocktails of antibiotics to prevent diseases from proliferating among their tightly packed livestock. Because livestock manure is used as fertilizer, drug-resistant bacteria are spreading within the soils and waterways of farms, contaminating even plant-producing environments. The result: a dramatic rise in drug-resistant bacterial infections, sickening two million people per year and killing 23,000 in the United States alone.

55. Which sentence best summarizes the passage's main idea?
    A) "The discovery of penicillin by Alexander Fleming in 1928 revolutionized medical care."
    B) "The widespread use of penicillin and other antibiotics has saved millions of people from the deadliest bacterial infections known to humans and prevented the spread of bacterial diseases."
    C) "But we have relied on antibiotics too heavily, which has undermined their effectiveness as bacteria evolve resistance to these drugs."
    D) "Because livestock manure is used as fertilizer, drug-resistant bacteria are spreading within the soils and waterways of farms, contaminating even plant-producing environments."

56. What is the meaning of the word *revolutionized* in the first sentence?
    A) rebelled and rejected authority
    B) protested unfair treatment
    C) inspired hopeful thoughts
    D) transformed and modernized

57. Which of the following is NOT listed as a detail in the passage?
    A) Factory farms give antibiotics to pigs, cattle, chickens, and turkeys.
    B) Factory farmers give their animals "cocktails of antibiotics"—more than one kind of antibiotics.
    C) On factory farms, livestock are packed closely together.
    D) On some farms, free-range chickens and turkeys can wander about the property.

58. What is the author's primary purpose in writing this essay?
    A) to suggest changing the ways we use antibiotics
    B) to suggest that people need to stop taking so many antibiotics
    C) to honor Alexander Fleming's groundbreaking discovery of penicillin
    D) to suggest that factory farmers need to start treating their animals more humanely

59. Readers can infer from reading this passage that the author feels ___ about the "dramatic rise in drug-resistant bacterial infections."
    A) relieved
    B) concerned
    C) infuriated
    D) enthralled

60. In the last sentence, what does the word *dramatic* mean?
    A) theatrical
    B) impressive
    C) thrilling
    D) striking

Mathematics

Directions: Work the problem, and then choose the most correct answer.

1. A patient weighs 110 pounds. What is her weight in kilograms?
    A) 55 kg
    B) 50 kg
    C) 11 kg
    D) 20 kg

2. Solve the following expression with $a = -10$:

$$\frac{a^2}{4 - 3a + 4}$$

   A) 26.32
   B) -4.54
   C) −45.45
   D) 2.63

3. A skateboarder is moving down the sidewalk at 15 feet per second. What is his approximate speed in miles per hour?
    A) 30.7 mph
    B) 22 mph
    C) 15.9 mph
    D) 10.2 mph

4. A patient has a condition that requires her to limit her fluid intake to 1,800 milliliters per day. A family member brings her a bottle of water that contains 591 milliliters, and she drinks the whole bottle. How many milliliters of water can the patient ingest the rest of the day?
   A) 1,391 ml
   B) 1,209 ml
   C) 2,391 ml
   D) 1309 ml

5. Solve: $12x + 5 = 77$
   A) −6
   B) 6
   C) 10
   D) 8

6. The dosage for a certain medication is 2 milligrams per kilogram. What dosage should be given to a patient weighing 165 pounds?
   A) 150 mg
   B) 250 mg
   C) 132 mg
   D) 50 mg

7. What is 40% of 124?
   A) 310
   B) 4.96
   C) 49.6
   D) 31

8. Solve the proportion: $\frac{5}{x} = \frac{7}{14}$
   A) 70
   B) 10
   C) 2.5
   D) 25

9. Which of the following numbers is the greatest?
   A) 0.29
   B) $\frac{2}{9}$
   C) $\frac{1}{4}$
   D) 0.26

10. Yuri's cell phone bill is computed using the formula $A = 50 + 0.15(x - 750)$, where x is the number of texts he sends for the month. Find the amount of Yuri's bill when he sends 820 texts.
    A) $173
    B) $60.50
    C) $123
    D) $39.50

Practice Test

11. What fraction is equivalent to 0.375?
    A) $\frac{37}{100}$
    B) $\frac{3}{8}$
    C) $\frac{2}{5}$
    D) $\frac{33}{4}$

12. Andre welded together three pieces of metal pipe, measuring 26.5 inches, 18.9 inches, and 35.1 inches. How long was the welded pipe?
    A) 10.3 in
    B) 80.5 in
    C) 27.5 in
    D) 42.7 in

13. The diameter of a round table is 60 inches. What is the diameter of the table in meters?
    A) 1.667 m
    B) 2.5 m
    C) 1.524 m
    D) 0.75 m

14. Simplify the following expression: $(5-2)3-14 \div 7$
    A) 2
    B) 25
    C) $-\frac{5}{7}$
    D) 7

15. One foot is approximately how many centimeters?
    A) 30.5 cm
    B) 5.08 cm
    C) 100 cm
    D) 45 cm

16. $(-9)(-4) =$
    A) −13
    B) 13
    C) −36
    D) 36

17. The electric company uses the formula $C = 0.057k + 23.50$, where k represents the number of kilowatt-hours used by the customer, to determine the amount of a customer's bill. Find the bill amount for a customer who uses 1,210 kilowatt-hours.
    A) $68.97
    B) $713.20
    C) $30.40
    D) $92.47

18. Solve: $5(x + 3) - 12 = 43$
    A) 8
    B) 12
    C) 9
    D) 10

19. 33 is 15% of what number?
    A) 33.15
    B) 165
    C) 220
    D) 48

20. The average high temperature in Paris, France, in July is 25°C. Convert the temperature to Fahrenheit.
    A) 13°F
    B) 43°F
    C) 77°F
    D) 57°F

21. The recommended dosage of a particular medication is 4 milliliters per 50 pounds of body weight. What is the recommended dosage for a person who weighs 175 pounds?
    A) 25 ml
    B) 140 ml
    C) 14 ml
    D) 28 ml

22. Put the following numbers in order from least to greatest: $-0.31, 0.25, -\frac{2}{5}, \frac{1}{3}$
    A) $0.25, -0.31, \frac{1}{3}, -\frac{2}{5}$
    B) $-0.31, -\frac{2}{5}, \frac{1}{3}, 0.25$
    C) $\frac{1}{3}, 0.25, -0.31, -\frac{2}{5}$
    D) $-\frac{2}{5}, -0.31, 0.25, \frac{1}{3}, \frac{1}{3}$

23. Normal body temperature is 98.6°F. Convert the temperature to Celsius.
    A) 37°C
    B) 54.8°C
    C) 66.6°C
    D) 47°C

Practice Test

24. Convert 0.46 to a fraction in lowest terms.
    A) $\frac{3}{500}$
    B) $\frac{23}{10}$
    C) $\frac{23}{50}$
    D) $\frac{2}{3}$

25. 23 + 19.09 + 4.7 =
    A) 19.79
    B) 24.02
    C) 26.09
    D) 46.79

26. A local supermarket is sponsoring a 10k (10 kilometer) run for charity. How many miles is the run?
    A) 16.1 mi
    B) 10 mi
    C) 5 mi
    D) 6.2 mi

27. Simplify the following expression: 2(7 − 9) + 4 × 10
    A) 36
    B) 44
    C) 0
    D) 160

28. One day in January, the low temperature was −7°F. During the day the temperature rose 15 degrees. What was the high temperature?
    A) −23°F
    B) 23°F
    C) −8°F
    D) 8°F

29. If Tim is driving 75 miles per hour, how far will he travel in 24 minutes?
    A) 187.5 mi
    B) 30 mi
    C) 24 mi
    D) 40 mi

30. A medication's expiration date has passed. The label says it contains 600 milligrams of ibuprofen, but it has lost 125 milligrams of ibuprofen. How much ibuprofen is left in the tablet?
    A) 475 mg
    B) 525 mg
    C) 425 mg
    D) 125 mg

31. Simplify the following expression: $2(3x + 4y) + 7(2x - 2y)$
   A) $20x - 6y$
   B) $5x + 2y$
   C) $20x^2 - 6y^2$
   D) $20x + 22y$

32. Solve: $\frac{x}{4} + \frac{2}{3} = \frac{29}{12}$
   A) 5
   B) 12
   C) 7
   D) 10

33. How much alcohol by volume is in a 500 milliliter bottle of 70% isopropyl alcohol?
   A) 35 ml
   B) 50 ml
   C) 400 ml
   D) 350 ml

34. If one serving of milk contains 280 milligrams of calcium, how much calcium is in 1.5 servings?
   A) 187 mg
   B) 295 mg
   C) 420 mg
   D) 200 mg

35. A pencil is 19 centimeters long. What is its approximate length in inches?
   A) 48.26 in
   B) 7.5 in
   C) 15 in
   D) 3.75 in

36. Fried's rule for computing an infant's dose of medication is: $\frac{\text{child's age in months} \times \text{adult dosage}}{150}$ If the adult dose is 25 milligrams, how much should be given to a one-and-a-half-year-old child?
   A) 3 mg
   B) 6 mg
   C) 4 mg
   D) 5 mg

37. Chan owes his parents $2,500. So far he has paid back $800. What percent of the original loan has Chan paid back?
   A) 68%
   B) 32%
   C) 16%
   D) 8%

38. If 2 tablets contain 600 milligrams of medicine, how much medicine is in half a tablet?
    A) 300 mg
    B) 150 mg
    C) 120 mg
    D) 1,200 mg

39. A doctor has prescribed Norco $\frac{10}{325}$, which contains 10 milligrams of hydrocodone and 325 milligrams of acetaminophen, to help control a patient's post-op pain. The warning on the prescription label cautions patients to limit their intake of acetaminophen to less than 3,500 milligrams per day. How many tablets can the patient take while staying under the daily limit?
    A) 9
    B) 10
    C) 11
    D) 12

40. If the average person drinks ten 8-ounce glasses of water each day, how many ounces of water will they drink in a week?
    A) 80 oz
    B) 700 oz
    C) 560 oz
    D) 70 oz

Science

1. Which of the following statements makes anatomical sense?
    A) The knees are superior to the shoulder.
    B) The stomach is lateral to the kidneys.
    C) The fingers are proximal to the shoulders.
    D) The urethral meatus is anterior to the anus.

2. Water molecules are considered polar because they
    A) form hydrogen bonds.
    B) are held together by a covalent bond.
    C) have a high specific heat.
    D) have partial positive and negative charges.

3. The identity of an element is determined by its number of
    A) neutrons.
    B) nuclei.
    C) protons.
    D) electrons.

4. Which chamber of the heart pumps deoxygenated blood to the lungs?
    A) right atrium
    B) right ventricle
    C) left atrium
    D) left ventricle

5. A race car accelerates from 0 miles per hour to 60 miles per hour in 4 seconds. What is the race car's acceleration?
    A) 6.7 m/s2
    B) 15.0 m/s2
    C) 15.7 m/s2
    D) 240.0 m/s2

6. Why do the tails of phospholipids not interact with water?
    A) The phospholipids' tails are too large to interact with water.
    B) Non-polar molecules do not interact with water.
    C) Inorganic molecules interact with each other.
    D) Water molecules have a high specific heat.

7. Which of the following describes a function of cilia in the trachea?
    A) They keep the windpipe clear by moving mucus up.
    B) They prevent food from entering the trachea.
    C) They produce mucus to trap contaminants.
    D) They produce sound as air moves over them.

8. Which of the following is found in plant cells but not in animal cells?
    A) cell wall
    B) Golgi apparatus
    C) plasma membrane
    D) proteins

9. Tay-Sachs disease is caused by a four-codon insertion that causes errors in the production of the enzyme beta-hexosaminidase. What kind of mutation causes Tay-Sachs disease?
    A) point mutation
    B) base substitution
    C) frameshift mutation
    D) deletion

10. Which of the following is a negatively charged subatomic particle?
    A) neutron
    B) proton
    C) cation
    D) electron

11. Which of the following tasks is performed by bones and joints?
    A) They store iron, calcium, and fat.
    B) They disintegrate old blood cells.
    C) They produce fluids for protection.
    D) They promote muscle growth.

12. Which molecule is produced during the Calvin cycle?
    A) carbon dioxide
    B) glucose
    C) water
    D) ATP

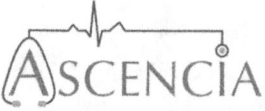

13. What magnitude of force does a 1 kilogram object exert on the surface of the earth?
    A) 0.10 N
    B) 0.98 N
    C) 9.8 N
    D) 98 N

14. Which of the following describes the path followed by sperm as it exits the body?
    A) vas deferens → epididymis → ejaculatory duct
    B) epididymis → seminiferous tubes → urethra
    C) seminiferous tubes → vas deferens → ejaculatory duct
    D) ejaculatory duct → vas deferens → penis

15. Which zone of the sarcomere has myosin filaments that are thick and do not shorten during muscle contraction?
    A) Z-line
    B) A-band
    C) I-band
    D) H-zone

16. To form nucleosomes, DNA is wrapped around
    A) histones.
    B) chromatin.
    C) centromeres.
    D) ATP.

17. How many electrons are needed to complete the valence shell of the halogens?
    A) 1
    B) 2
    C) 6
    D) 7

18. Which type of neuron controls the movement of voluntary muscles?
    A) sensory neurons
    B) visceral afferent neurons
    C) interneurons
    D) efferent neurons

19. Cystic fibrosis is a recessive trait. If the mother does not carry the recessive gene, but the father carries a single copy, what are the chances that their child will have cystic fibrosis?
    A) 0 percent
    B) 25 percent
    C) 50 percent
    D) 75 percent

20. In which phase of the cell cycle do chromosomes become visible?
    A) S
    B) G2
    C) interphase
    D) prophase

134   Practice Test

21. How much kinetic energy does a 0.14-kilogram baseball have if it is pitched at 100 miles per hour?
    A) 3.24 J
    B) 145 J
    C) 324 J
    D) 14,486 J

22. Which layer of the stomach has cells that secrete hydrochloric acid and digestive enzymes?
    A) serosa
    B) submucosa
    C) muscularis
    D) mucosa

23. What type of bond is formed between one positively charged atom and one negatively charged atom?
    A) ionic bond
    B) hydrogen bond
    C) covalent bond
    D) metallic bond

24. Which of the following is produced during transcription?
    A) DNA
    B) mRNA
    C) lipids
    D) proteins

25. Which of the following is a response by the innate immune system when tissue is damaged?
    A) The skin dries out.
    B) The temperature increases.
    C) The blood flow to the area decreases.
    D) The heart rate slows.

26. What is the gravitational potential energy stored in a 2.5 gram penny held over the edge of a building that is 400 meters tall?
    A) 9.8 J
    B) 98 J
    C) 980 J
    D) 9,800 J

27. Where are the adrenal glands found?
    A) in the brain
    B) on the back of the thyroid
    C) on the kidneys
    D) in the pelvic area

28. Which of the following is a chemical property?
    A) viscosity
    B) density
    C) toxicity
    D) color

29. Which of the following is a carbohydrate?
    A) DNA polymerase
    B) vegetable oil
    C) fructose
    D) mRNA

30. What state of matter has a definite shape and definite volume?
    A) solid
    B) liquid
    C) gas
    D) plasma

31. A mover exerts a constant 400 newton force to push a sofa up a 10 meter-long truck ramp. How much work does the mover do?
    A) 40 J
    B) 400 J
    C) 4,000 J
    D) 40,000 J

32. Which of the following hormones is released by the kidneys and helps regulate blood pressure?
    A) renin
    B) calcitriol
    C) cortisol
    D) oxytocin

33. Which organelle produces energy in the form of ATP?
    A) mitochondria
    B) nucleus
    C) vacuole
    D) Golgi apparatus

34. Which of the following secretes progesterone and estradiol after the egg is fertilized?
    A) oocyte
    B) corpus luteum
    C) fallopian tube
    D) fimbriae

35. The purpose of oxygen in the electron transport chain is to
    A) form water.
    B) drive the proton gradient.
    C) act as the final electron acceptor.
    D) carry protons.

36. What constant force is required to act on a 1 kilogram mass to do 850 joules of work over a distance of 100 meters?
    A) 0.85 N
    B) 8.5 N
    C) 85 N
    D) 850 N

37. What role do the sinoatrial (SA) and atrioventricular (AV) nodes play in the circulatory system?
    A) They control the amount of blood that enters the heart's chambers.
    B) They produce fluid to lubricate the heart's muscles.
    C) They coordinate the contraction of the atria and ventricles.
    D) They repair injured muscle tissue around the heart.

38. Orange juice is primarily composed of citric acid and malic acid. Which of the following is most likely its pH?
    A) 4
    B) 7
    C) 9
    D) 13

39. How many nucleotides are in a codon?
    A) 3
    B) 4
    C) 5
    D) 6

40. Which layer of the skin contains large numbers of blood vessels?
    A) epidermis
    B) dermis
    C) hypodermis
    D) subcutaneous

42. A rope with one end attached to a wall is shaken up and down. Visually, this is an example of what type of wave?
    A) mechanical
    B) electromagnetic
    C) longitudinal
    D) transverse

43. A patient has recently been diagnosed with a bone marrow disorder that leads to slow blood clotting. The patient is likely low in which of the following?
    A) red blood cells
    B) plasma
    C) platelets
    D) hemoglobin

44. What are the coefficients needed to balance the equation below?

$$\_Pb(NO_3)_2 + \_K_2CrO_4 \rightarrow \_PbCrO_4 + \_KNO_3$$

    A) 1, 1, 1, 2
    B) 2, 2, 2, 3
    C) 1, 1, 1, 1
    D) 3, 3, 3, 1

Practice Test

45. Which of the following is an important function of the pleural cavity?
    A) It allows the lungs to expand.
    B) It protects the lungs from the ribcage.
    C) It produces fluid to protect the lungs.
    D) It supports the diaphragm.

46. In which phase of mitosis do homologous chromosomes separate?
    A) interphase
    B) prophase
    C) anaphase
    D) metaphase

47. Letting go of a compressed spring transmits what type of visual wave?
    A) mechanical
    B) electromagnetic
    C) longitudinal
    D) transverse

48. What is a function of antibodies during an immune response?
    A) They store information for antibody production when the antigen reappears.
    B) They ingest the pathogen and destroy it.
    C) They produce an enzyme to coat and protect healthy cells.
    D) They bind to the antigen to neutralize pathogens.

49. A pickup truck applies a constant 500 newton meters of torque to an axle with a radius of 10 centimeters. What perpendicular force acts on the axle?
    A) 50 N
    B) 500 N
    C) 5,000 N
    D) 50,000 N

50. Which of the following mixtures is heterogeneous?
    A) coffee with sugar
    B) orange juice with pulp
    C) hot tea
    D) purified water

51. Which is the final phase of mitosis?
    A) interphase
    B) metaphase
    C) anaphase
    D) telophase

52. Which ATP-producing pathway occurs in the cytoplasm?
    A) Krebs cycle
    B) glycolysis
    C) photosynthesis
    D) Calvin cycle

53. What is the relationship between the pressure in the lungs and the movement of air out of the lungs?
    A) Negative pressure in the lungs moves the air out.
    B) Positive pressure in the lungs moves the air out.
    C) Neutral pressure in the lungs moves the air out.
    D) Decreasing pressure in the lungs moves the air out.

54. In plants, what does the Calvin cycle do?
    A) convert CO2 into a sugar
    B) produce ATP when light is not available
    C) use the energy in light to split water into hydrogen and oxygen
    D) generate ATP, NADPH, and oxygen

55. Which of the following is a waste product that results from protein catabolism?
    A) uric acid
    B) urea
    C) nitrates
    D) phosphates

56. Which of the following particles is found in the nucleus of an atom?
    A) neutron
    B) valence electron
    C) core electron
    D) photon

57. Which process do cells use to produce ATP when oxygen availability is low?
    A) Krebs cycle
    B) fermentation
    C) glycolysis
    D) electron transport chain

58. What is the role of the thyroid gland?
    A) It controls the release of hormones from the pituitary gland.
    B) It regulates the sleep cycle.
    C) It controls the body's metabolic rate.
    D) It regulates blood sugar level.

59. Which molecule is used as the final electron acceptor during fermentation?
    A) glucose
    B) pyruvate
    C) oxygen
    D) carbon dioxide

60. How much time does it take a 100 watt light bulb to do 100 joules of work?
    A) 0.01 s
    B) 1 s
    C) 100 s
    D) 1 hour

Answer Key

Verbal Skills

1. C: Apathetic means "indifferent."

2. A: Belligerent means "hostile."

3. B: Callous means "insensitive."

4. D: Hinder means "impede."

5. B: Lucid means "rational" or "clear."

6. A: Pilfering means "stealing."

7. C: Inconspicuous means "unnoticeable."

8. A: Frantic means "frenzied."

9. C: Exacerbated means "aggravated" or "to make something worse."

10. D: Verbose means "wordy."

11. D: To foster means "to promote."

12. A: To quantify is "to measure" or "count the value of something."

13. D: The first paragraph begins with "Most people think…." The author goes on to describe external respiration and then asks, "Did you know there are actually two types of respiration in humans?" Finally, the author describes the other type: internal respiration. The author is probably correct in assuming that most people—excluding biologists and medical professionals—have never heard of internal respiration.

14. C: As the title shows, the passage is about the two types of respiration: external and internal.

15. A: In paragraph 2, the author writes, "Whereas external respiration centers on an exchange between the lungs and the environment, internal respiration centers on a molecular exchange between cells and capillaries."

16. A: The primary purpose of the essay is to inform; its focus is on the two types of respiration. It is not persuasive or advisory. The author is not trying to prove a point.

17. C: In the second paragraph, the author writes, "Additionally, built-up carbon dioxide in the tissues flows through the capillaries back to the lungs."

18. D: In paragraph 2, the author writes, "Cells within the organs are surrounded by thousands of tiny capillaries that act as channels for the exchange of gases. Oxygen is carried through these microscopic blood vessels, moving from red blood cells to the surrounding tissue." Readers can infer from context that the phrase "these microscopic blood vessels" refers to the "thousands of tiny capillaries" in the previous sentence.

19. D: The last sentence provides an adequate summary of the passage. The other sentences provide specific details from the passage.

20. B: Beginning in 1733 and continuing through the present day, the author explains how blood pressure measuring techniques and instruments have evolved.

21. C: In the second paragraph, the author writes, "In 1896, Italian physician Scipione RivaRocci ... created what we still recognize as a sphygmomanometer, the conventional blood pressure meter that we use today."

22. C: In the first paragraph, the author describes an invasive procedure used to measure animals' blood pressure. In the second paragraph, the author writes, "Fortunately, we no longer have to use such invasive methods to study blood pressure." The author thinks it is a good thing that blood pressure can be measured less invasively.

23. B: The author writes, "Even though we now also have digital methods that do not use mercury, blood pressure is still described in millimeters of mercury (mm Hg)." There are no sentences supporting the other claims.

24. B: In the third paragraph, the author writes, "The cuff of the sphygmomanometer is placed around the patient's upper arm and tightened enough to stop the blood flow."

25. B: In the second paragraph, the author writes, "If you are waiting until you are thirsty to anSwer key 145drink something, then you are already dehydrated; our thirst mechanism fails to 'notify' our body of dehydration in time." There is no support for any of the other claims.

26. C: In the third paragraph, the author writes, "The amount of water an individual needs varies based on such factors as metabolism or diet, but conventional wisdom is that humans should take in anywhere between 2.7 and 3.7 liters of water each day." Readers can infer that by "conventional wisdom," the author means the standard advice that medical professionals give their patients.

27. C: The primary purpose of the essay is to explain; its general focus is on dehydration. It is not primarily cautionary or advisory. The author does not tell a story about a specific patient.

28. C: In the first sentence, the author writes, "Water accounts for roughly 60 percent of an adult human's body weight and is essential for most bodily functions." Readers can infer from context that the phrase "essential for most bodily functions" means that without water, the body could not function—so water is crucial for "most bodily functions."

29. D: The passage defines dehydration and details its causes, possible effects, and prevention. The other sentences give details from the passage.

30. A: In the first paragraph, the author writes, "Dehydration ... can be caused by illness, exercise, heat, stress, or lack of self-care."

31. C: The passage does not contain this detail. According to the passage, smoking e-cigarettes may cause "popcorn lung," but the author does not identify this disorder as lung cancer.

32. B: The text is informative, not persuasive or reassuring. Probably the author wants readers to be aware that the harmful effects of e-cigarettes are still not clear.

33. C: In the first sentence, the author writes, "E-cigarettes have only been around for about fifteen years, but they are a booming business." In the last sentence, the author refers to "the growth of the e-

Answer Key

cigarette business." The context shows that by "booming business" the author means that the e-cigarette business is very successful: many consumers have bought this product.

34. C: In the first paragraph, the author writes, "E-cigarettes...contain a liquid that is heated to produce an aerosol that is then inhaled. The liquid usually contains nicotine, the primary addictive substance in tobacco." Readers can infer that, since e-cigarettes usually contain an addictive substance (nicotine), they are usually addictive.

35. B: In the second paragraph, the author states, "Other medical professionals believe e-cigarettes may, in fact, help [the war on smoking tobacco] by providing smokers with an alternative to smoking tobacco, which, in addition to nicotine, contains many harmful substances and is unequivocally linked with multiple types of cancer." The reader can infer from this information that the author thinks it is good to quit smoking tobacco, since scientists know for sure that tobacco is harmful and causes cancer.

36. D: The passage is mainly about an ongoing debate over the pros and cons of e-cigarettes. The author points out that research has raised more questions rather than provide answers. The other answer choices provide details from the passage.

37. B: The author writes that, due to new studies that show it can take up to six months to fully heal from a concussion, school districts and doctors may now advise that an injured student athlete wait much longer than just two weeks—perhaps a full six months—before returning to play.

38. B: In the second paragraph, the author writes, "The brain is commonly known for its fragility; ironically, it may be its resiliency that is hiding the long-term effects of concussions. A concussion is a mild traumatic brain injury. The brain is tremendously resilient in how it deals with the damage: it can 'rewire' around the area of trauma and make new neurological connections." The context shows that the author uses the words resiliency and resilient to refer to the brain's ability to heal itself quickly.

39. B: The passage does not contain this detail. The passage does not mention school coaches' role in deciding when injured athletes must or should start playing again.

40. B: The author points out that new studies have shown that, following a concussion, the brain may take up to six months to heal completely. The passage deals primarily with implications for school athletes.

41. A: In the first paragraph, the author writes, "New studies indicate that the impact of a single concussion, even if it is a person's first, can cause longer-lasting neurological damage than we previously knew—possibly even permanent."

42. C: In the first sentence, the author writes, "New studies indicate that the impact of a single concussion, even if it is a person's first, can cause longer-lasting neurological damage than we previously knew." In the second paragraph, the author writes, "A concussion is a mild traumatic brain injury." Readers can infer that neurology is the study of the human brain and nervous system.

43. B: In the first paragraph, the author writes, "Pain is a highly sophisticated biological mechanism, one that is often downplayed or misinterpreted. Pain is much more than a measure of tissue damage—it is a complex neurological chain reaction that sends sensory data to the brain."

44. B: In the third paragraph, the author writes, "Phantom pain, most commonly associated with the amputation or loss of a limb, ... is triggered even in the absence of any injury. One possible explanation is that the spinal cord is still processing sensations from that area."

45. A: The passage is mainly about the fact that pain is a complicated process. The other sentences provide details from the passage.

46. D: In paragraph 3, the author writes, "Phantom pain may be caused when the spinal cord continues to process sensations from that area."

47. A: In the first paragraph, the author writes, "Pain...is a complex neurological chain reaction that sends sensory data to the brain."

48. A: In the last paragraph, the author writes, "The absence of pain...is a double-edged sword—sometimes pain is the only clue to an underlying injury or disease. Likewise, an injury or disease can dull or eliminate pain, making it impossible to sense when something is actually wrong." Readers can infer that the author is using the metaphor of a double-edged sword to show that the absence of pain is not always positive.

49. B: The passage is mainly about the composition of snake venom. The other sentences give details from the passage.

50. C: In the last paragraph, the author writes, "Researchers have been studying the chemical compositions of these venoms and have been making strides in using the science behind the toxins to combat major diseases such as cancer, heart disease, and Alzheimer's." Readers can infer that the author is using the phrase "making strides in using the science" to refer to making discoveries that greatly improve medical science's ability to cure diseases.

51. D: In the last sentence in the second paragraph, the author writes, "Some cytotoxins target specific types of cells—myotoxins affect muscles, cardiotoxins attack the heart, and nephrotoxins damage the kidneys." Readers can infer that *myo* refers to muscles, *cardio* refers to the heart, and *nephro* refers to the kidneys, as in nephritis (inflammation of the kidneys).

52. A: In the first paragraph, the author writes, "The two key ingredients in all snake venoms are enzymes and polypeptides. Some enzymes help the snake disable its prey, and others help the snake digest its prey." Later in the passage the author goes into more detail about these processes.

53. C: The primary purpose of the essay is to inform; its general focus is on the composition of snake venoms. It is not primarily cautionary or advisory. The author does not tell a story about a specific research scientist.

54. B: In the first sentence, the author writes, "Many snakes produce a toxic fluid in their salivary glands called venom." Readers can infer from this that some snakes do not produce venom. There is no support for any of the other claims.

55. C: The passage is mainly about ways that the overuse of antibiotics has led drug-resistant bacteria to evolve. The other sentences give details from the passage.

56. D: In the first sentence, the author writes, "The discovery of penicillin by Alexander Fleming in 1928 revolutionized medical care. The widespread use of penicillin and other antibiotics has saved millions of people from the deadliest bacterial infections known to humans and prevented the spread of bacterial diseases." The context shows that the author uses the word revolutionized to refer to an important discovery that modernized medicine and saved many lives.

57. D: The passage does not contain this detail. The passage does not mention other types of farms besides factory farms.

Answer Key

58. A: While the author does not explicitly suggest a solution, he or she points out a serious problem that is caused by using antibiotics in harmful ways.

59. B: Phrases such as "undermined their effectiveness," "inundating [livestock] with cocktails of antibiotics," "dramatic rise in drug-resistant infections," and "sickening two million people per year and killing 23,000 in the United States alone" show that the author feels very concerned about the problem described in the passage.

60. D: In the last two sentences, the author writes, "Because livestock manure is used as fertilizer, drug-resistant bacteria are spreading within the soils and waterways of farms, contaminating even plant producing environments. The result: a dramatic rise in drug-resistant bacterial infections, sickening two million people per year and killing 23,000 in the United States alone." Readers can infer that by "a dramatic rise," the author means "a very noticeable or striking rise."

Mathematics

1. B:

$$110 \text{ lb} \times \frac{1 \text{ kg}}{2.2 \text{ lb}} = 50 \text{ kg}$$

2. D:

$$\frac{(-10)^2}{4 - 3(-10) + 4}$$

$$\frac{100}{4 + 30 + 4} =$$

$$\frac{100}{38}$$

$$= 2.63$$

3. D:

$$\frac{15 \text{ ft}}{\text{sec}} \times \frac{3{,}600 \text{ sec}}{1 \text{ hr}} \times \frac{1 \text{ mi}}{5{,}280 \text{ ft}} \approx 10.2 \text{ mph}$$

4. B:

$$1{,}800 - 591 = 1{,}209$$

5. B:

$$12x + 5 = 77$$
$$12x = 72$$
$$x = 6$$

6. A:

$$\frac{2 \text{ mg}}{\text{kg}} \times \frac{1 \text{ kg}}{2.2 \text{ lb}} \times 165 \text{ lb} = 150 \text{ mg}$$

7. C:
$$\text{part} = \text{whole} \times \text{percent}$$
$$124 \times 0.40 = 49.6$$

8. B:
$$\frac{5}{x} = \frac{7}{14} \quad 7x = 70 \quad x = 10$$

9. A:
$$\frac{2}{9} = 0.\overline{2}$$
$$\frac{1}{4} = 0.25$$
$$0.29 > 0.26 > 0.25 > 0.22$$

10. B:
$$50 + 0.15(820 - 750)$$
$$50 + 0.15(70)$$
$$50 + 10.50 = 60.50$$

11. B:
$$375 \div \frac{125}{1{,}000} \div 125 = \frac{3}{8}$$

12. B:
$$26.5 + 18.9 + 35.1 = 80.5$$

13. C:
$$60 \text{ in} \times \frac{2.54 \text{ cm}}{\text{in}} \times \frac{1 \text{ m}}{100 \text{ cm}} = 1.524 \text{ m}$$

14. B:
$$(5 - 2)^3 - 14 \div 7$$
$$= 33 - 14 \div 7$$
$$= 27 - 2 = 25$$

15. A:
$$1 \text{ ft} \times \frac{12 \text{ in}}{\text{ft}} \times \frac{2.54 \text{ cm}}{\text{in}} = 30.48 \text{ cm} \approx 30.5 \text{ cm}$$

16. D:
$$\text{negative} \times \text{negative} = \text{positive} \quad (-9)(-4) = 36$$

17. D:
$$0.057(1{,}210) + 23.50 = 68.97 + 23.50 = 92.47$$

Answer Key

18. A:

$$5(x + 3) - 12 = 43$$
$$5x + 15 - 12 = 43$$
$$5x + 3 = 43$$
$$5x = 40$$
$$x = 8$$

19. C:

$$\text{whole} = \frac{\text{part}}{\text{percent}}$$
$$\frac{33}{0.15} = 220$$

20. C:

$$F = 1.8C + 32$$
$$F = 1.8(25) + 32$$
$$F = 77°$$

21. C:

$$\frac{4}{50} = \frac{x}{175}$$
$$50x = 700$$
$$x = 14$$

22. D:

$$-\frac{2}{5} = -0.4$$
$$\frac{1}{3} = 0.\overline{3}$$
$$-0.4 < -0.31 < 0.25 < 0.3$$

23. A:

$$C = \frac{5}{9}(F - 32)$$
$$C = \frac{5}{9}(98.6 - 32)$$
$$C = \frac{5}{9}(66.6) = 37°$$

24. C:

$$\frac{46 \div 2}{100 \div 2} = \frac{23}{50}$$

25. D:
$$23 + 19.09 + 4.7 = 46.79$$

26. D:
$$10 \text{ km} \times \frac{1 \text{ mi}}{1.61 \text{ km}} \approx 6.2 \text{ mi}$$

27. A:
$$2(7-9) + 4 \times 10$$
$$= 2(-2) + 4 \times 10$$
$$= -4 + 4 \times 10$$
$$= -4 + 40 = 36$$

28. D:
$$-7 + 15 = 8$$

29. B:
$$\frac{75 \text{ mi}}{\text{hr}} \times \frac{1 \text{ hr}}{60 \text{ min}} \times 24 \text{ min} = 30 \text{ mi}$$

30. A:
$$600 - 125 = 475$$

31. A:
$$2(3x + 4y) + 7(2x - 2y)$$
$$6x + 8y + 14x - 14y$$
$$6x + 14x + 8y - 14y$$
$$20x - 6y$$

32. C: Multiply by the least common denominator to clear the fractions.
$$(12)\frac{x}{4} + (12)\frac{2}{3} = (12)\frac{29}{12}$$
$$3x + 8 = 29$$
$$3x = 21$$
$$x = 7$$

33. D:
$$\text{part} = \text{whole} \times \text{percent}$$
$$500 \times 0.70 = 350$$

34. C:
$$\frac{1}{280} = \frac{1.5}{x}$$
$$x = 420$$

Answer Key

35. B:

$$19 \text{ cm} \times \frac{1 \text{ in}}{2.54 \text{ cm}} \approx 7.5 \text{ in}$$

36. A:

$$1\frac{1}{2} \text{ years} = 18 \text{ months}$$

$$\frac{18 \times 25}{150}$$

37. B:

$$\text{percent} = \frac{\text{part}}{\text{whole}}$$

$$\frac{800}{2,500} = 0.32 = 32\%$$

38. B:

$$\frac{2}{600} = \frac{0.5}{x}$$

$$2x = 300$$

$$x = 150$$

39. B:

$$3,500 \div 325 \approx 10.8$$

So, 10 tablets will stay under the limit.

40. C:

$$1 \text{ week} = 7 \text{ days} \quad 10 \times 8 \times 7 = 560$$

Science

1. D: The urethral meatus is toward the front, or anterior, relative to the anus.

2. D: The electrons in a water molecule are more attracted to the oxygen atom, which gives the oxygen atom a negative charge and the hydrogen atoms a positive charge.

3. C: The number of protons determines which element it is.

4. B: Deoxygenated blood in the heart is delivered to the lungs for gas exchange from the right ventricle.

5. A: Convert 60 miles per hour to meters per second. Plug the variables into the appropriate formula and solve for acceleration.

$$\frac{60 \text{ mi}}{\text{hr}} \times \frac{1,609 \text{ m}}{1 \text{ mi}} \times \frac{1 \text{ hr}}{3,600 \text{ sec}} = 26.8 \frac{\text{m}}{\text{s}}$$

6. B: The fatty acid tails of phospholipids are non-polar, and non-polar molecules are repelled by water and other polar molecules.

7. A: The cilia help move the mucus up to keep the trachea clear.

8. A: Both plant and animal cells have carbohydrates, nucleic acids, proteins, and lipids. Plants and animals have similar organelles, including the Golgi apparatus. However, plant cells have a cell wall, whereas animal cells do not.

9. C: In a frameshift mutation, insertions of nucleotides in numbers other than three will shift all the following codons read by the tRNA, producing a dysfunctional protein. 10.

10. D: Electrons are negatively charged subatomic particles. 11.

11. A: The bones and joints store iron, calcium, and fat.

12. B: The Calvin cycle is the part of photosynthesis where ATP is used to convert CO_2 and water to sugar.

13. C: Plug the variables into the appropriate formula and solve.

$$Fg = mg$$
$$Fg_g^g = 1 \text{ kg}(9.8 \frac{m}{s^2}) = 9.8 \text{ N}$$

14. C: Sperm travels from the seminiferous tubes through the vas deferens to the ejaculatory duct.

15. B: The A-band has thick myosin filaments that do not shorten with muscular contraction.

16. A: DNA is organized into chromosomes using histone proteins. First, DNA is wound into nucleosomes by histones. Next, the nucleosomes are wound into chromatin, which is wound even tighter to form chromosomes.

17 B: is correct. The fatty acid tails of phospholipids are non-polar, and non-polar molecules are repelled by water and other polar molecules.

18. D: Efferent neurons control the movement of voluntary muscles.

19. A: Because cystic fibrosis is a recessive trait, the offspring would have to inherit two recessive alleles in order to have the disorder. Since the mother can only pass on dominant alleles, all of the children will have at least one dominant allele and thus will not have cystic fibrosis.

		Mother	
		C	C
Father	C	CC	CC
	c	Cc	Cc

20. D: During prophase, the nuclear envelope disappears and the chromosomes begin to condense into chromatin, which makes them visible with a light microscope.

21. B: Convert 100 miles per hour to meters per second.

$$\frac{100 \text{ mi}}{\text{hr}} \times \frac{1{,}609 \text{ m}}{\text{mi}} \times \frac{1 \text{ hr}}{3{,}600 \text{ s}} = 44.7 \frac{m}{s}$$

Answer Key

Plug the variables into the appropriate formula and solve.

$$KE = \frac{1}{2}mv^2$$

$$KE = \frac{1}{2}(0.145 \text{ kg})\left(44.7\frac{m}{s}\right)^2 = 145 \text{ J}$$

22. D: The mucosa is the innermost layer of the stomach; it secretes hydrochloric acid and digestive enzymes.

23. A: Ionic bonds contain an atom that has lost electrons to the other atom, which results in a positive charge on one atom and a negative charge on the other atom.

24. B: Transcription is the process of converting DNA into mRNA so that the genetic code (DNA) can be translated into protein on ribosomes.

25. B: Inflammation increases the blood flow to the damaged area, increasing the temperature and bringing white blood cells to the site.

26. A: Plug the variables into the appropriate formula and solve.

$$PE = mgh$$

$$PE_g^g = (0.0025\text{kg})\left(9.8\frac{m}{s^2}\right)(400 \text{ m}) = 9.8 \text{ J}$$

27. C: Adrenal glands are found on top of each kidney.

28. C: Toxicity is a chemical property: measuring the toxicity of a material will change its chemical identity.

29. C: Carbohydrates, such as fructose, are sugars. DNA polymerase is a protein, vegetable oil is a lipid, and mRNA is a nucleic acid.

30. A: A solid has a definite shape and definite volume.

31. C: Plug the variable into the appropriate formula and solve:

$$W = Fd$$

$$W = (400 \text{ N})(10 \text{ m}) = 4{,}000 \text{ J}$$

32. A: Renin is released by the kidneys and plays a role in regulating blood pressure.

33. A: Mitochondria produce energy for cells in the form of ATP. The electron transport chain, which is responsible for most of the ATP produced during respiration, occurs across the membranes of the mitochondria.

34. B: The corpus luteum, which remains in the ovary after the egg is released, produces progesterone and estradiol after the egg is fertilized in the fallopian tube.

35. C: Oxygen acts as the final electron acceptor during the electron transport chain. In the process of making energy (ATP), ATP synthase passes electrons on to oxygen.

7. A: The cilia help move the mucus up to keep the trachea clear.

8. A: Both plant and animal cells have carbohydrates, nucleic acids, proteins, and lipids. Plants and animals have similar organelles, including the Golgi apparatus. However, plant cells have a cell wall, whereas animal cells do not.

9. C: In a frameshift mutation, insertions of nucleotides in numbers other than three will shift all the following codons read by the tRNA, producing a dysfunctional protein. 10.

10. D: Electrons are negatively charged subatomic particles. 11.

11. A: The bones and joints store iron, calcium, and fat.

12. B: The Calvin cycle is the part of photosynthesis where ATP is used to convert CO_2 and water to sugar.

13. C: Plug the variables into the appropriate formula and solve.

$$Fg = mg$$
$$Fg_g^g = 1 \text{ kg}(9.8\frac{m}{s^2}) = 9.8 \text{ N}$$

14. C: Sperm travels from the seminiferous tubes through the vas deferens to the ejaculatory duct.

15. B: The A-band has thick myosin filaments that do not shorten with muscular contraction.

16. A: DNA is organized into chromosomes using histone proteins. First, DNA is wound into nucleosomes by histones. Next, the nucleosomes are wound into chromatin, which is wound even tighter to form chromosomes.

17 B: is correct. The fatty acid tails of phospholipids are non-polar, and non-polar molecules are repelled by water and other polar molecules.

18. D: Efferent neurons control the movement of voluntary muscles.

19. A: Because cystic fibrosis is a recessive trait, the offspring would have to inherit two recessive alleles in order to have the disorder. Since the mother can only pass on dominant alleles, all of the children will have at least one dominant allele and thus will not have cystic fibrosis.

		Mother	
		C	C
Father	C	CC	CC
	c	Cc	Cc

20. D: During prophase, the nuclear envelope disappears and the chromosomes begin to condense into chromatin, which makes them visible with a light microscope.

21. B: Convert 100 miles per hour to meters per second.

$$\frac{100 \text{ mi}}{\text{hr}} \times \frac{1,609 \text{ m}}{\text{mi}} \times \frac{1 \text{ hr}}{3,600 \text{ s}} = 44.7 \frac{m}{s}$$

Plug the variables into the appropriate formula and solve.

$$KE = \frac{1}{2}mv^2$$

$$KE = \frac{1}{2}(0.145 \text{ kg})\left(44.7\frac{m}{s}\right)^2 = 145 \text{ J}$$

22. D: The mucosa is the innermost layer of the stomach; it secretes hydrochloric acid and digestive enzymes.

23. A: Ionic bonds contain an atom that has lost electrons to the other atom, which results in a positive charge on one atom and a negative charge on the other atom.

24. B: Transcription is the process of converting DNA into mRNA so that the genetic code (DNA) can be translated into protein on ribosomes.

25. B: Inflammation increases the blood flow to the damaged area, increasing the temperature and bringing white blood cells to the site.

26. A: Plug the variables into the appropriate formula and solve.

$$PE = mgh$$

$$PE_g^g = (0.0025 \text{ kg})\left(9.8\frac{m}{s^2}\right)(400 \text{ m}) = 9.8 \text{ J}$$

27. C: Adrenal glands are found on top of each kidney.

28. C: Toxicity is a chemical property: measuring the toxicity of a material will change its chemical identity.

29. C: Carbohydrates, such as fructose, are sugars. DNA polymerase is a protein, vegetable oil is a lipid, and mRNA is a nucleic acid.

30. A: A solid has a definite shape and definite volume.

31. C: Plug the variable into the appropriate formula and solve:

$$W = Fd$$

$$W = (400 \text{ N})(10 \text{ m}) = 4{,}000 \text{ J}$$

32. A: Renin is released by the kidneys and plays a role in regulating blood pressure.

33. A: Mitochondria produce energy for cells in the form of ATP. The electron transport chain, which is responsible for most of the ATP produced during respiration, occurs across the membranes of the mitochondria.

34. B: The corpus luteum, which remains in the ovary after the egg is released, produces progesterone and estradiol after the egg is fertilized in the fallopian tube.

35. C: Oxygen acts as the final electron acceptor during the electron transport chain. In the process of making energy (ATP), ATP synthase passes electrons on to oxygen.

36. B: Plug the variables into the appropriate formula and solve:

$$W = Fd$$

$$F = \frac{W}{d}$$

$$F = \frac{850 \text{ J}}{100 \text{ m}} = 8.5 \text{ N}$$

37. C: The sinoatrial (SA) and atrioventricular (AV) nodes are cells that coordinate the pace and contraction of the heart.

38. A: Acids have a pH between 0 and 7

39. A: Each codon contains three nucleotides.

40. B: The dermis is the layer of the skin where blood vessels, hair follicles, and glands are found.

41. D: At the beginning of telophase I, homologous chromosomes are located at opposite ends of the cell. As telophase I progresses, the 2n cell divides into two cells with a reduced number (1n) of chromosomes.

42. D: A shaken rope is in the form of a transverse wave. 43.

43. C: Platelets, also known as thrombocytes, play an important role in blood clotting.

44. A: The balanced equation is:

$$Pb(NO_3)_2 + K_2CrO_4 \rightarrow PbCrO_4 + 2KNO_3$$

This shows 1Pb, $2NO_3$, 2K, and $1CrO_4$ on each side of the arrow. The answer choice is 1, 1, 1, 2.

45. A: The pleural cavity provides a space for the lungs to expand.

46. C: Chromosomes are separated to opposite ends of the cell during anaphase.

47. C: A relaxing spring visually transmits longitudinal waves.

48. D: Antibodies bind to the antigen on the pathogen, neutralizing the pathogen and attracting phagocytes.

49. C: Plug the variables into the appropriate formula and solve.

50. B: Orange juice contains bits of solid pulp that are not uniformly spread out, making it a heterogeneous mixture. heterogeneous mixture.

51. D: Telophase is the final phase of mitosis. Telophase is the final phase of mitosis.

52. B: Glycolysis is the energy-producing pathway that occurs in the cell's cytoplasm.

53. B: Positive pressure in the lungs will move air out of the lungs.

54. A: The Calvin cycle is the biochemical pathway that converts CO2 into sugar.

55. B: Urea is the result of protein catabolism.

56. A: The nucleus contains protons and neutrons. All electrons are found outside the nucleus, and photons are packets of electromagnetic waves that can be emitted or absorbed by an electron.

57. B: Fermentation occurs when oxygen levels are low.

Answer Key

58. C: The thyroid gland controls the use of energy by the body.

59. B: During fermentation, pyruvate is used as the final electron acceptor when oxygen levels are low.

60. B: Plug the variables into the appropriate formula and solve.

ONLINE RESOURCES

Trivium includes online resources with the purchase of this study guide to help you fully prepare for the exam.

Practice Test

In addition to the practice test included in this book, we also offer an online exam. Since many exams today are computer based, practicing your test-taking skills on the computer is a great way to prepare.

Review Questions

Need more practice? Our review questions use a variety of formats to help you memorize key terms and concepts.

Flash Cards

Trivium's flash cards allow you to review important terms easily on your computer or smartphone.

Cheat Sheets

Review the core skills you need to master the exam with easy-to-read Cheat Sheets.

From Stress to Success

Watch "From Stress to Success," a brief but insightful YouTube video that offers the tips, tricks, and secrets experts use to score higher on the exam.

Feedback

Let us know what you think!

Access these materials at: ascenciatestprep.com/nex-online-resources

Dear NEX test taker,

Great job completing this study guide. The hard work and effort you put into your test preparation will help you succeed on your upcoming NEX exam. Thank you for letting us be a part of your education journey!

We have other study guides and products that you may find useful. Search for us on Amazon.com or let us know what you are looking for. We offer a wide variety of study guides that cover a multitude of subjects.

If you would like to share your success stories with us, or if you have a suggestion, comment, or concern, please send us an email at support@triviumtestprep.com.

Thanks again for choosing us!
Happy Testing
Ascencia Test Prep Team